# HOW TO
# CHOOSE
# A HUSBAND

# HOW TO CHOOSE

# A HUSBAND

*and make peace with marriage*

## Suzanne Venker

 WND Books

# HOW TO CHOOSE A HUSBAND

WND Books
Washington, D.C.

Copyright © 2013
Suzanne Venker

Book designed by Mark Karis

WND Books are distributed to the trade by:
Midpoint Trade Books
27 West 20th Street, Suite 1102
New York, New York 10011

WND Books are available at special discounts for bulk purchases. WND Books, Inc.,
also publishes books in electronic formats. For more information call
(541) 474-1776 or visit www.wndbooks.com.

First Edition

Hardcover ISBN: 978-1936488582
eBook ISBN: 978-1936488957

Library of Congress information available

Printed in the United States of America
10 9 8 7 6 5 4 3 2 1

*for Emma*

May you find someone just like Daddy.

The first time.


*and for Henry*

May you find a woman who lives an examined life.

# Table of Contents

*Change your thoughts
and you change your world.*

—Norman Vincent Peale

*Acknowledgments*

I'VE ALWAYS BEEN ENVIOUS of authors who refer to their editors as friends. Finally, I can do the same. Words cannot convey my gratitude to Megan Byrd—our introduction was positively serendipitous. Thank you, thank you, thank you, MB . . . for getting it. And thank you for your stellar editorial skills; your way cool personality; your outstanding work ethic; and most of all, your friendship. I still have to remind myself you're only twenty-seven.

I am also blessed to have artist extraordinaire Mark Karis on my side—as well as publishers Joseph and Elizabeth Farah. WND Books is a gem, and I'm honored to be among its list of exceptional writers.

And of course there would be no Megan, or Mark, or WND Books, if there were no Bill. Thank you, my dear, for patiently leading me to them. And thank you for being the man you are. I feel so safe with you it's ridiculous.

Finally, I'd like to recognize the silent warriors who've helped push me along in the face of adversity—and there are many, from my family and friends to my readers and general supporters of my work. Thank you, Mom, for loving everything I write. (You do realize you're hopelessly biased, don't you?) Thank you to Sam as well, who changed my perspective 100 percent. Thank you Sarah and Cathy, for *everything*. And finally, a great big thank you to my longtime friends, Katie and Ruthie. I'm so blessed to have you both in my corner.

Onward!

# *What this book is not*

W HEN PEOPLE HEARD I was writing a book called *How to Choose a Husband*, they'd say something like this to my husband, Bill: "Wow, that must make you feel great!" Perhaps it does, but with all due respect to my husband—who is, admittedly, a great man—this book is not about how Suzanne Venker hit the jackpot and how you, too, can find your very own Bill. Our marriage is just like everyone else's: it's full of ups and downs, loaded with conflicts and, left unchecked, potentially combustible.

It's supposed to be. It's a marriage.

*How to Choose a Husband* is not pretty talk. It is not your personal overnight guide to getting a ring, nor will it help you find the perfect husband or marriage. I have neither. *No one does.* What I do have is a husband who believes, as I do, that we must work with what we've got. And that has made all the difference in the world.

Perhaps somewhere in existence there *are* couples who ride off into the sunset and mesh beautifully along the way. Perhaps they never fight or even disagree. Perhaps they have fabulous sex day in and day out, no matter what life throws them. But if these couples exist, I've never met them.

Too many people want marriage to be something it's not; and when it doesn't measure up, they become antsy and dissatisfied. Some have affairs, and some get divorced—all in search of something better, something more meaningful, or something more exciting. But if you want a certain kind of marriage, it doesn't just happen. You have to be willing to create it.

I don't have all the answers, but this much I *can* tell you: whether or not you are happily married will dictate the entire course of your life. It will measure the flow of your days, be the determiner of your children's well-being, even color your view of the world. You will take a good marriage or a bad marriage with you everywhere you go. It is the barometer for everything else you do.

With that in mind, I want you to think about all the time and energy you've spent preparing for and/or pursuing a career. Now imagine if you spent even half that time and energy preparing to become a wife. You know, like women used to do.

Sound crazy? Silly? Something only our grandmothers did? Perhaps. But our grandmothers found husbands and kept them.

Have you?

*What this book is*

H OW TO CHOOSE A HUSBAND can change your life. Really. I wrote it for the woman who feels alone in her desire to get married and settle down, who's looking for The One but getting nowhere, who thinks she's found The One but wants to be sure, who's living with her boyfriend and suffering from inertia, who's divorced but would like to remarry, who's considering divorce but has yet to pull the trigger, or who's still single at thirty-five and wishes she weren't.

You are not the problem. Society is.

How could you *not* be struggling? Unlike every other generation in history, yours was taught to postpone marriage indefinitely or ignore it altogether, as though marriage had no bearing on your happiness. As though it were a nice idea, or nice accompaniment to an otherwise satisfying life. This message has been so strong for so long that it's now chic to be single. "Living alone comports with modern values. It promotes freedom, personal control, and self-realization—all prized aspects of contemporary life," wrote Eric Klinenberg, author of *Flying Solo*.[1]

But if flying solo is so great, why are businesses like Match.com, eHarmony, Spark, and It's Just Lunch booming with clients looking to get hitched? Sure, being single is fun—for a while. But most people don't want to stay single. Men and women are irrevocably drawn to one another. Since the beginning of time, this attraction has been the driving force of our survival as a species—and until recent decades has almost always resulted in lasting marriage. But somewhere along the line, we lost our way.

*How to Choose a Husband* presents a very different message from the one you've gleaned from the culture. You will read things here that sound utterly foreign and may even make you cringe. *Do not despair.* Simply hold your breath, and carry on. Because if you're a young woman—say, anywhere between eighteen and thirty-five—you have hit the jackpot. And if you're over thirty-five and still searching for Mr. Right, or if you're married and you *wish* your husband were Mr. Right, you, too, may have hit the jackpot.

I should warn you, though: that's not how the media will describe this book. They'll say *How to Choose a Husband* suggests we should all go back to the '50s. *That is not my message.* But what has happened to marriage over the past half century can hardly be called progress. Perhaps the more accurate way to describe my position is that I believe women have robbed Peter to pay Paul.

It will also be tempting to assume that since I place much of the blame for what has happened to marriage on women, I think men, as a whole, are innocent. That is not what I think. Of course there are bad men/ husbands/fathers in the world. But this book isn't about them. *If you are a woman who's involved with, or married to, a man who's abusive; has an active addiction; is mentally unstable; or is generally unable to think, act, and behave like a married man, this is not the book for you.* Such relationships fall into a different category and require professional guidance. *How to Choose a Husband* offers guidance of a different sort.

First, the underlying problem: modern women are living in a culture that isn't the least bit interested in helping them get hitched. The cultural messages about life and love are poisonous. The most lethal is the idea that there's an easy answer to everything. Finding a fiancé and building a lasting relationship is supposed to be as easy as picking out a box of cereal in the grocery store. Simply choose the one you want, throw it in the cart, and you're good to go. That's certainly the message of *The Bachelor* and *The Bachelorette.*

But that's not how it works. No matter how pretty you are, no matter how much money you have, no matter how talented you may be, you will never find a perfect marriage, wrapped with a red bow, on your doorstep.

Mr. Right is not going to appear as a result of all the work you've put in to bettering yourself. Men may be attracted to beauty and brilliance, but they're far less concerned with your career success than you are. What matters most is character and kindness.

To find Mr. Right, you must first understand what men want. Once you have that down (and you will after you read this book), you'll need to be *very intentional* about whom you choose to marry. Because getting married isn't a decision you're going to make once. From the moment you slide that ring on your finger, you will have to choose your husband over and over again—every day of your life. If you want to stay married, that is.

You also need to recognize your enemy. The culture is working against you every step of the way, and knowing this will go a long way toward helping ward off potential disaster. At the moment, the single greatest problem your generation faces is the relentless anti-male/pro-female rhetoric you're exposed to. It's inescapable.

As an example—and, believe me, there are thousands from which to choose—in the June 2012 issue of *Marie Claire*, Rebecca Traister wrote: "The world as we've known it for a very long time—one in which a woman's value was tied to her role as a wife—is ending, right in front of us. It is now standard for a woman to spend years on her own, learning, working, earning, socializing, having sex, and yes, having babies in the manner she—and she alone—sees fit. We are living through the invention of independent female adulthood."[2]

This message—that women don't need men or marriage—is palpable and toxic. America is simply not interested in helping you find lasting love. If it were, we would honor the marriage relationship. We would embrace the unique qualities men and women bring to the table and foster an environment that helps bring the sexes together. But we don't. We honor sex, singlehood, and female empowerment. How on earth, then, are you supposed to find a husband and keep him around for the long haul?

That's what this book is about.

I'm sure you've heard the phrase "Marriage is work." That's true, but it's too cliché. A better way to explain it is that marriage isn't something you get, like a reward for being a good girlfriend. Marriage is something you *do*. It's a vocation. The reason people call it work is because, as a wife, you will need to make a clear and purposeful choice to love someone even when you don't feel like it. Even when your problems seem insurmountable or when your spouse doesn't deserve it. That's because marriage is about learning how to love someone in spite of yourself. In spite of the fact that sometimes you won't feel warm fuzzies for your husband, or you may want to bolt, or you're just going to be plain old unhappy.

And here's a newsflash: your husband's going to feel the *exact same way*.

That's a hard pill to swallow since your generation, the women in particular, have been raised to believe they're entitled to be happy all the time. What a liability! No one can be happy all the time. If you want to know true liberation, chuck the idea that you're supposed to be fulfilled every waking moment. You're not. It's no wonder your generation is always disappointed: your expectations don't align with reality. If the goal is to get married and stay married, you're going to have to change your entire outlook on men and marriage. There's no way around it.

I know you can do it because I did. When I found myself divorced at twenty-seven (no kids), I had a come-to-Jesus party. I was forced to reevaluate what happened and why. In the *Wall Street Journal*, Elizabeth Bernstein wrote about a recent study that tracked divorcées' advice on marriage, "People who lose the most important relationship of their life tend to spend time thinking about what went wrong. If they're at all self-reflective, this means they will acknowledge their own mistakes, not just their ex's blunders."[3]

I can assure you I've spent a very long time doing just that. My past haunted me for years. Immediately following my divorce, in 1995, I spent one soul-searching year living like a hermit in a town on the New Jersey/Pennsylvania border that I'd visited once and haven't seen since. I eventually moved back home to the Midwest, where I met and married my second husband. He and I have been married almost fifteen years; and we have two children, ages ten and thirteen.

But here's the thing. While I made a better choice for myself the second time around, that doesn't mean I can sit back and relax. My husband and I aren't exempt from problems just because we make a good match. For one thing, we both bring a lot of baggage to our marriage—which people tend to do when they marry in their thirties (or even late twenties). Nowadays people have romantic pasts that for many included cohabitation or, in my case, marriage. This is a marked difference between the younger and older generations. We simply have more on our plates.

What this means is that marriage is no longer a simple arrangement. People don't grow up, fall in love, get married, and pop out a few bambinos. Life is more complicated.

How did it happen?

In a phrase, the *sexual revolution*. This social movement was a momentous turning point in American history. Under the guise of equality, women were sold a script about sex and gender roles—one they've been hanging on to ever since. The underlying theme was the idea that women can, and should, have sex like a man: without getting attached. But as Lena Dunham of the hit HBO series *Girls* told Frank Bruni of the *New York Times*, this cultural expectation conflicts with human nature. Despite the chorus of sexual liberation that's been drilled into the women of Dunham's generation, the twenty-six-year-old producer/actress finds the message counterintuitive.

"I heard so many of my friends saying, 'Why can't I have sex and feel nothing?' It was amazing: that this was the new goal. There's a biological reason why women feel about sex the way *they* do and why men feel about sex the way they do. It's not as simple as divesting yourself of your gender roles."[4]

Indeed it isn't. But today's marriage-minded woman is up against a new America: one so hopelessly vacuous it believes living alone, earning a paycheck, and choosing sex over love is superior to the sacrifices and rewards of marriage and family life. Hanna Rosin, author of *The End of Men and the Rise of Women*, describes the new ethos this way: "Thanks to the sexual revolution, [women] can have relationships—and maybe some drama—through their twenties and early thirties and not get tied down with a husband and babies. If the price is a little more heartache, so be it. These days women have a lot more important things on their horizon."[5]

Go ahead—read that again. I'll wait.

Are you back? How on earth can women get it right when they've absorbed this elitist, self-serving crap since the day they were born? Ms. Rosin is wrong. The price of the sexual revolution is not "a little more heartache." It's a boatload. For most women, at their core, nothing is more important than finding Mr. Right. Nothing.

Nevertheless, women like Rosin—a.k.a. feminists with clout—have made it their mission to try to eradicate male and female nature. Because of this, the feminist worldview is the only frame of reference modern women have when it comes to sex, marriage, and gender roles. And what have they learned? That with the exception of their private parts, men and women are virtually indistinguishable. But that's a whole different concept of equality. Being equal in worth, or value, is not the same as being identical, interchangeable beings.

If you're old enough, or if you have older siblings, you may recall the album *Free to Be You and Me* and its accompanying illustrated book. It was produced in 1972 by Marlo Thomas and her like-minded friends in Hollywood. It was a hugely successful album, in part because the songs were so much fun to sing and the characters were too cute for words.

But *Free to Be You and Me* was more than a record album. It was a project with a name: the Free to Be Foundation. This foundation is a subsidiary of the Ms. Foundation for Women, which was founded by Thomas's dear friend and feminist icon Gloria Steinem. The seemingly benign *Free to Be* album was part and parcel of the feminist movement, or what you probably refer to as the "women's movement."

The album's creators had a specific goal in mind: to eradicate any semblance of sexual stereotyping. In the song/skit "Boy Meets Girl," writers Carl Reiner and Peter Stone were asked to counteract "conventional myths about the differences between boys and girls." So they came up with this: Two babies, a male and a female, have just been born and are "sitting" side by side in their respective cribs. They each note that they look and feel the same, particularly since their heads are bald. Then the baby boy announces he wants to be a cocktail waitress when he grows up, and the baby girl says she wants to be a fireman. It isn't until the nurse changes each baby's diaper that the babies realize which gender they really are. The moral of the story is that the only thing separating males and females is their private parts.

The message of every song on the *Free to Be* album is some variation of this same theme. The implication is that for a man to be a real man, he should drop the macho behavior and get in touch with his feminine side. As for women, there's no such thing as a biological desire to be cared for by a man, or even to procreate. Besides, marriage and motherhood hold women back. (Remember Princess Atalanta?) They keep women from realizing their true potential. *Free to Be You and Me* wasn't some innocuous album; it was a tool feminists used to reach American families.

And it worked.

For more than four decades, feminist ideology has become an integral part of life for Western women. Girls in America and across the ocean are raised differently than any other generation of women. They're taught to never rely on a man; that their lives should be "me-centered" rather than "others-centered"; and that enlightened women are career-driven and should, at the very least, be ambivalent about becoming wives and mothers.

Just to be clear, I'm not suggesting feminism is *solely* to blame for the changes that have occurred in courtship and marriage. Rampant materialism certainly plays a role, as do the decline in religion and the rise of a one-click culture—none of which foster the patience and sacrifice that is a staple of married life. They also make it difficult for young people to see beyond tomorrow, which is imperative for making good decisions. The self-esteem movement is another culprit.

But of all the changes that have occurred in the last half century, it is feminism—with its relentless talk of hapless housewives, female empowerment, and gender role reversal—that has severed the bond between the sexes, making it almost impossible for young people to navigate the dating scene and wind up happily married.

Today, marriage is considered passé. I've personally heard more than one boomer-age parent tell me their daughters say they're never getting married. That isn't surprising—look at their role models. As the caption on the January 2012 cover story of *Boston Magazine*, entitled "Single by Choice," reads, "This is Terri. She's successful, happy, and at 38, just fine with never getting married. Ever."[6]

But these daughters who are so adamantly opposed to marriage now will wake up from their fog one day. They will, as we say, grow up. And when they do, they will be despondent about having harbored such views. Don't get me wrong: the modern generation's reticence about marriage is real and understandable. But it is fear, not indifference to marriage, that's motivating them. Women *want* to move forward. They just don't know how.

The "You Go, Girl" world in which they've been raised goes completely counter to the life of a wife and mother. It is downright daunting to reconcile the reality of marriage, which demands selflessness and capitulation (on the part of both spouses) with a worldview that extols female autonomy. Add to this juxtaposition a narcissistic culture, and Americans have conjured the perfect storm. Consider these comments on the *The Huffington Post* by singer/songwriter Rachel Fine, twenty-nine, regarding her upcoming nuptials:

> I don't know why, but I've always identified strongly as a very independent woman. I've always thrived in a man's world, and to do that, you almost have to shut off your girlie side. I'm starting to think there may be a whole generation of chicks like me who grew up with "Free to Be . . . You and Me" on repeat and are now having a tough time embracing their inner girlie-ness.
>
> The idea of excelling at any type of domestic-type activity always had a Taming of the Shrew vibe to me. As if cooking my man a pot roast would somehow invite the destruction of my inner being via a 50-foot Godzilla version of Donna Reed. And, seriously, this underlying belief system has been in place since kindergarten.[7]

Just as unfortunate are women who missed the marriage boat altogether and are struggling to understand their predicament. Consider these comments made by Kate Bolick, whose article about the single life was featured on the front page of *The Atlantic.*

> The decision to end a relationship for abstract reasons, rather than for concrete reasons ("something was missing"), I see now, is in keeping with a post-Boomer ideology that values emotional fulfillment above all else. And the elevation of independence over coupling ("I wasn't ready to settle down") is a second-wave feminist idea I'd acquired from my mother, who had embraced it, in part, I suspect, to correct for her own choices.
>
> I was her first and only recruit, marching off to third grade in tiny green or blue t-shirt declaring: A Woman Without a Man Is Like a Fish Without a Bicycle and bellowing along to Gloria Steinem & Co.'s feminist-minded children's album, Free to Be . . . You and Me.[8]

Kate Bolick and Rachel Fine are not anomalies. They represent an entire generation (two, actually) who've been raised to view marriage as a disastrous undertaking. They've been taught that marriage will not add to their lives but will take something of value away. Being someone's wife will destroy their most cherished values—freedom and independence—and replace them with . . . nothing.

Well, shoot, who'd want to get married when you put it that way?

Compounding the problem is that so many members of Generations X and Y were raised in broken homes. As a result, they have no idea what a good marriage looks like. Susan Gregory Thomas, author of *In Spite of Everything,* is a great example. Thomas's parents split when she was twelve, and in an article about her book, she lamented the lack of guidance available to young people. "Why would we take counsel," she asked, "from the very people who, in our view, flubbed it all up?"[9]

You wouldn't—unless those same individuals were introspective enough to admit where they went wrong. In that case, you might learn a lot. But the previous generation of American women is saturated with feminist thinkers. And they tend to be a bitter lot, as Ms. Bolick's story demonstrates.

Nothing about our postfeminist culture is helpful for building strong marriages. On the contrary, American women have become resentful and suspicious of men—which perpetuates the divorce cycle. Despite insisting she would never do to her children what her parents did to her, Thomas and her husband got divorced. "I don't know what makes a good marriage," she wrote.[10]

And that, of course, is the crux of the problem. If the modern generation doesn't know what makes a good marriage, how can they possibly know what to look for in a mate? How in the world are women supposed to navigate the dating scene, find Mr. Right, and settle down in a culture hell-bent on steering them in a different direction?

There's only one way: a detox.

A detox, you may know, is the process an addict goes through when he wants to rid himself of toxins that have invaded his body. Our postfeminist culture is toxic. It celebrates women at the exclusion of men; it ignores the needs of children; and it glorifies the single life. That's not going to help you in the least.

Sadly, more women than not will allow this poison to invade their bodies and even ruin their lives. But you don't have to. There are three steps involved in any detox:

1. Recognize the problem.
2. Rid your body of the toxins.
3. Give your body the healthy nutrients it craves.

In other words, you must recondition your brain to think about marriage in a way that contradicts everything you've been taught since the day you were born. *There is nothing wrong with wanting to get married and have babies.* It's the most natural desire in the world. You are not any less strong, capable, or intelligent as a woman for wanting to do so. There is no reason you can't be a woman in your own right and still be a wife and mother. You can even take your husband's name and combine bank accounts!

I know this sounds Pollyanna-ish, but honestly: the answer lies in your attitude.

*Part One*

# YOU GO, GIRL!

*It had seeped into their minds like intravenous saline into the arm of an unconscious patient. They were feminists without knowing it.*

—Danielle Crittenden

# *1*

# THE NAKED EMPEROR

WHENEVER I TALK TO WOMEN in their twenties and thirties about feminism, it usually falls on deaf ears. To most of them, feminism was just some movement when women burned their bras and fought for women's rights. The details escape them. But what these women do know, or *think* they know, is that they owe their lives to the women (i.e., feminists) who came before them. After all, that's what they've been told over and over and over again.

But let's set the record straight: You don't owe feminists anything.

Feminism isn't what you think it is. It is, in fact, a radical movement and ideology—though it has never been billed as such. Rather, it is sold as something any enlightened human being would embrace. The assumption is that, if it weren't for feminists, women in America would be second-class citizens. They'd be stuck in secretarial jobs or at home doing the grunt work of caring for the house and kids while men got to lead exciting lives in the marketplace.

That many women got college degrees and worked outside the home before the 1960s (my mother and grandmother—who was born in the *nineteenth century*—included) goes unmentioned. That men, once they marry, are also bound to family obligations and make sacrifices of a different sort goes unchallenged as well. For years, feminists have assured women it is they who've suffered the most.

Have you ever read the Hans Christian Andersen story "The Emperor's New Clothes"? I'm always reminded of it when I think about feminism's influence on society and what might happen if people were privy to the facts.

A vain emperor who cares only about his appearance hires two tailors who are, in fact, swindlers. They promise the emperor the finest clothes, made from a fabric that's invisible to those too dense to see it. The emperor can't see the cloth himself but pretends he can out of fear of appearing stupid. When the swindlers finish making the suit, the emperor marches in procession before his subjects, who play along with the pretense.

Suddenly, a child in the crowd, too young to understand the desirability of keeping up the pretense, shouts that the emperor is wearing nothing at all! Then the crowd admits they don't see anything either. The emperor cringes with embarrassment, but continues with the procession—vowing never to be swindled again.

Feminists, in effect, are swindlers. Their agenda is made up of, well, not *nothing* exactly, but bits and pieces of truth that are sewn together in such a way that the end result is a fabrication that sounds perfectly reasonable. A great example is equal pay for equal work. Sounds benign, doesn't it? Who *wouldn't* believe in getting paid for work you've actually performed? But that's just it: women don't make as much as men precisely *because* they don't work the same number of hours. Women continue to take years off the job to care for their children, or aging parents, or to live a more balanced life. Feminists leave that part out.

Working motherhood is another example. Feminists love to tell Americans that most mothers today are "working mothers." But they don't define this term. Instead, they choose to lump all mothers who bring home *any income at all* as "working mothers"—even though there's a clear distinction between mothers who work sixty or eighty hours a week while their toddlers are in other women's care, and mothers who work twenty hours a week while their older children are in school. That's why feminists are swindlers: they take a grain of truth and spin the hell out of it.

Many people also associate feminism with the right to vote. That's because feminists claimed their movement was a continuation, or "part two," of an earlier movement: the suffragettes' fight for the female vote. (This fight began in the nineteenth century, and by 1920, American women secured the right to vote in all fifty states.) By piggybacking off that earlier movement, feminism is classified as first-, second-, or third-wave feminism. The first wave is associated with the female vote; the second wave is associated with the sexual revolution; and the third wave refers to modern-day feminism, which is even more radical.

In reality, the feminist movement has little in common with the suffragette movement. Suffragettes, for example, were anti-abortion. But by putting the two together, it was easy for feminists to gain traction. After all, any normal person thinks women should vote. Ergo, "equal rights for women," the platform of the 1960s feminist revolution, must be a good thing, too.

But any serious study of feminism—there are a copious number of books, articles, and films if you're interested—reveals startling truths and commonalities among its leaders. For instance, they also had very dysfunctional upbringings, fraught with emotional abuse or neglect. Many had mothers who resented them or their fathers; and feminists, understandably, internalized this dysfunction as children. Here's a direct quote from Gloria Steinem: "I didn't understand the degree to which my response has been magnetized by things that had happened to me before—and I think that realization came out of being depressed."[1]

When women like Steinem grew up, they displaced their pain onto society. Instead of putting their personal stories in context, with each woman understanding that her mother's unhappiness was just that—*her* unhappiness—they concluded their mothers weren't to blame for their problems. They figured that if society had functioned the way it was supposed to in the first place—with men and women as interchangeable genders—their mothers would have been happy. Harboring this attitude allows women to resent their mothers less and hate men more. See how it works?

As to the changes that have occurred with gender roles, it's true more women run companies today and more fathers change diapers—which is all well and good. It's also true feminism may have forced this along. But it was an inevitable phenomenon, as technological changes continue to provide opportunities for women that didn't exist before.

In almost every era, technology has provided women with the means to an easier life. In the 1940s, it was the washing machine; in the 1960s, it was the birth control pill; in the 1990s, it was the Internet. (Others inventions included the sewing machine, the frozen foods process, the automobile, etc.) All of these advancements—which were created by *men*, I might add—made life at home far less taxing.

Technology, not feminism, is what liberated women from household drudgery. Technology gave women what they've always craved: time. The more time women got, the more they began to enter the workforce. And the more women joined the workforce, the more husbands started taking on an active role at home.

Still, these changes haven't amounted to a full-scale gender role reversal because human nature doesn't change. After all this time, women still choose the caregiving professions (nursing, teaching, etc.) far more than men; and men still choose the physical and dangerous jobs (climbing trees and tall buildings, going into dark alleys with guns to confront bad guys) far more than women. Women also still choose to be their children's primary caregivers, while men choose to be their families' primary bread-winners. "The vast majority of at-home parents are still mothers," wrote Sharyn Alfonsi of ABC News.[2]

As I've already mentioned, I'm sure you've heard the media boast that the majority of mothers are now in the workforce. What they don't tell you is that only a minority of these women are employed full-time and year-round. Most mothers in America with children at home are either unem-ployed or employed part-time, or they move in and out of the workforce as the needs of their children change. They're not *at all* the depiction of the "working mother" you see on television. That's the script the media sells to the public to make women feel as if there's something wrong with them if their lives don't look like those of the women in the media. Remember the Hilary Rosen/Ann Romney debacle? That's a great example.

You've probably also heard over and over that mothers today "have to work." But the impetus for the exodus of mothers from the home had nothing to do with economics. It was the result of the relentless status degradation of the full-time homemaker/at-home mother. Simply put, women were sold on the idea that by staying home to take care of the house and children, their lives would be meaningless. They'd inevitably "lose themselves" in the process.

In fact, the shift away from mothers at home toward mothers at work is part and parcel of a larger cultural shift—away from family and onto the self, away from sacrifice and toward materialism. Today, women map out their lives according to this new set of values and then get "stuck" later, financially speaking, when it comes time to decide whether or not to stay home.

That's not the same thing as "having to work," as though someone or something thrust the situation upon them—like when my grandmother had to go to work after my grandfather was laid off during the Depression. We simply created a new economic model. The "having to work" argument doesn't even make sense: as a nation we used to be much poorer, and most mothers managed to stay home.

That isn't to say there aren't mothers in the workforce who must be there—that 41 percent of mothers in this country are single is evidence enough—but this doesn't make the facts about how we got here any less true. In the past, being a wife and mother was a noble vocation. In modern America, marriage + motherhood = jail. "I'd always had this feeling that if you got married, it was like the end of who you were,"[3] Sandra Bullock told Barbara Walters in a March 2010 interview. This attitude is now commonplace. Even men have jumped on board.

The saddest part of the whole thing is that marriage has been on a downward, not upward, spiral since the push for faux equality began. Feminists assured women their efforts would result in more satisfying, equitable marriages—but that has not happened. Instead, one of three things takes place.

(1) Women postpone marriage indefinitely, and move in and out of intense romantic relationships, or even live with their boyfriends. Eventually, their clocks start ticking and many decide they better hurry up and get married to provide a stable home for their yet-to-be-born children. Trouble is, they can't find a man who's willing to commit.

(2) Marriage becomes a competitive sport. The complementary nature of marriage—in which two people work together, as equals, toward the same goal but with an appreciation for the unique qualities each gender brings to the table—has been obliterated. Today, husbands and wives are locked in a battle about who does more on the home front and how they're going to get everything done. That's not a marriage. That's war.

(3) No-fault divorce, which feminists wholeheartedly support, makes ending one's marriage a piece of cake. Just check the "irreconcilable differences" box and pack your bags.

So I'll ask you: do you still think women are indebted to feminism?

.

## 2

# NEVER RELY ON A MAN

O F ALL THE MESSAGES FEMINISTS SENT, the most egregious
was the one they encouraged mothers to pass on to their
daughters: never depend on a man. The mothers who
pounded this home did so for one reason: their own relationships with
men—either their fathers or husbands, sometimes both—were fraught
with turmoil, just like the lives of feminist leaders. In such circumstances,
feminism becomes a convenient way to stay mad at the entire male popula-
tion—and then pass on this dysfunction to one's daughters.

Here's what you need to ask yourself. Was your mother's advice about
men and marriage of a positive or negative nature? If it was negative, ask
yourself why. Was your mother *really* a victim of her circumstances? Was
her father or husband—your grandfather or father—one of the bad guys,
thus tainting her view of men and marriage? That's certainly possible. But
it's just as possible your mother didn't choose the right husband and/or
do what was necessary to have a healthy, committed relationship. It's just
as possible her own life plans got derailed because of poor choices she
made along the way.

How you sort all this out is crucial because it'll put your mother's
advice in context. You may determine that she is, at heart, an unhappy
woman—or just a glass-half-empty kind of person. If that's the case, I'm
afraid her advice isn't going to help you. So the next thing you need to do

is forget all the negative vibes she sent forth about marriage and mother-hood. No matter how hard it is, accept that your mother doesn't have the answers you're looking for.

You don't have to be like her.

The truth is, the previous generation of American mothers did their daughters a great disservice. They were wrong to tell their daughters never to rely on a man. Harboring this attitude undermines a marriage before it even gets off the ground, just as telling a woman to keep her own name does. Both set up a negative right off the bat. They say, "Okay, I'll marry you, but I'm not in this thing 100 percent. You and the kids can represent the family unit, but I'm going to retain a separate identity. If I don't, being a wife and mother will swallow me whole."

This doesn't have to be your story. There are countless ways to achieve an identity outside of marriage. A job is one; but hobbies are great, too. So are volunteering and community involvement. These things are under-rated, of course, since America doesn't value work that doesn't provide a paycheck. But such pursuits are enormously satisfying. They instill in people a sense of purpose, one that is often lacking in the marketplace.

There's a difference, though, between making time for yourself—by leaving your kids with a sitter while you exercise, shop, have a few cocktails, or even work a part-time job—and becoming so absorbed in the pursuit of a career that the needs of your family don't get met. And there's simply no question that the pursuit of a demanding career is considered the only way a woman can retain her identity as a wife and mother.

It's time to put that message in the dumpster, where it belongs. Get-ting married and having children *will not* chip away at your identity. It will enhance it. It *could* chip away at it, I suppose—if you let it. So don't let it. *You do not need to become a harried working mother to prove your worthiness.*

As for men, I'm sure there are some husbands who don't pull their weight at home or who want their wives to be docile and obedient. I guess. Somewhere. But I've never met one. To assume most husbands are sus-ceptible to such thinking is absurd. Unless you made an exceptionally bad choice, like marrying a former convict from the backwoods, this is not going to be your fate. Most men are much nicer than you've been led to believe.

And most aren't threatened by a woman with power. *They care only when this power gets used against them or the marriage relationship.* That's where the problem lies today. There's nothing wrong with being successful in the marketplace. Where women get into trouble is when they bring their empowered selves home. When they walk in the door and forget to take off their boss hat.

Marriage isn't a power struggle; it's a partnership. Unless your husband's a Neanderthal—in which case, why'd you marry him in the first place?—he's not the least bit interested in seizing your identity. Most men don't want a doormat for a wife. One of the greatest ironies of feminism is that it never even occurs to the average husband to do the thing his wife is steeling herself against. In most cases, all that energy spent putting up a shield is for naught.

It's true that *motherhood* will curtail your independence; babies are totally dependent creatures. But life is about trade-offs. You can't have everything you want exactly the way you want it all the time. When you gain in one area, you lose in another. What goes up must come down. This is a law of physics you can't do anything about. And trust me: you'll feel positively liberated if you accept this truism rather than fight it.

Here's another fact that may surprise you. Most women find they *want* to stay home with their babies when they become mothers, despite the culture pulling them in the other direction. It's human nature to want to care for your own children. Which means the smart thing to do when mapping out your future is to assume the opposite of what your mother told you. Assume you *will* want, and need, to depend on a husband at some point. His job will allow you to care for your children, for however long you choose, without having to worry about producing an income. It's a wonderful give-and-take between husband and wife.

But you have to be open to it.

Of course, many couples switch things up—she works; he stays home—but most women want to take care of their children themselves, especially their babies. And most men, at least the good ones, would happily provide the means to allow this to happen. As jarring as it sounds, fathers have a vested interest in their children, too. Being products of divorce, many men today didn't have a mother at home and wish they had. Consequently, they would like their own children to have what they didn't have. But men have no voice in America. They can't ask, let alone expect, their wives to stay home. Not in a million years.

On the other side of the fence are the men who bought into feminist gobbledygook. They, too, have been pressured and cajoled into thinking educated women shouldn't "lower" themselves to taking care of babies. I can't tell you how many women I've heard from who want to know how they can convince their husbands that staying home is the right thing to do. These women aren't just fighting their mothers and the culture. They're fighting their own husbands! That we now have a country in which mothers have to *justify their desire* to care for their own babies speaks volumes. It's tragic.

But it makes sense, doesn't it? After all, men were sold the same script women were. They, too, absorbed the message that men and women are essentially the same. And since most men don't feel an innate pull to care for newborns around the clock, why would women? With this group, biology is totally dismissed.

Men have also been sold on the idea that babies can thrive in daycare. In one article I wrote about the importance of staying home, a male commenter had this to say: "Education is a tough thing to waste, Suzanne, particularly when you've spent so much of your money, your parents [*sic*] money, (and with financial aid/grants) full-tuition paying students/taxpayer's money to get it. To then 'stay home' and 'raise children' after spending all that money, well, I could see why that would anger some people. I could see where some might call that a very selfish thing to do. I'm sorry if you can't see that."[1]

I find this mind-boggling. Is there anything more selfless than raising children? To be fair, this man's comment is unusual. Most men I hear from fully understand the social and economic value of parenting. Still, they don't feel comfortable asking their wives to stay home or talking about this topic in public. They know if they did, they'd be branded sexists. That these fathers just want what's best for their children doesn't matter. Just *thinking* such a thing dubs a man a chauvinist.

What I don't want for you is to end up like those women in the magazines—the ones who are highly educated and successful in their field but whose home lives are a mess. Working mothers blame employers, husbands, even God for why they can't find balance in their lives. Time is their real enemy, but they don't see it that way. They bought into the myth that femininity is something to be squelched. They bought into the lie that happiness and contentment lie outside the home, not inside. They bought into all that junk that a woman shouldn't have to cook for or take care of a man. Today's women are enlightened! They're men's equals! They don't have to do any of that stuff.

What a load of crap. Every stinkin' last bit of it. Crap, crap, and more crap. Crapola personified. Being a strong, independent woman and being a wife and mother are *not* mutually exclusive. And cooking for a husband, or simply taking care of him out of love and respect, does not in any way diminish your needs or rights as a woman.

Shocking as it seems, it's rather rewarding.

## *3*

# SLUTVILLE

I F I WERE THE GAMBLING TYPE, I'd put money on the fact that you know many women who've slept with more guys than they can count. I know I do. I'm not sure how I managed to escape all that. I've just always felt sleeping with someone for the fun of it is a colossally stupid idea. Plus I've been relationship-oriented from the get-go.

As you know, women have been told this behavior is somehow liberating. For years feminists have assured women that "hooking up" (the more palatable term for acting like a slut) demonstrates a woman's self-confidence. What bunk. To willingly let countless men have their way with you, or to have sex with one's friends ("friends with benefits") is in fact proclaiming how *little* you think of yourself.

When it comes to sexuality, American women have engaged in a gigantic social experiment, and the damage has been profound. Some learn the lesson about casual sex after a sordid night or two, while others don't begin to understand or even acknowledge the ramifications for years—when it's often too late. What makes the message so insidious is that young women are prone to feeling insecure and are thus vulnerable to the idea that sleeping with a guy will make them more attractive. But I assure you the women my age who fell into this trap are mortified about their past behavior. And to those who feel otherwise, I would ask this: Are you going to suggest your daughters do the same thing? (Or your sons, for that matter?)

What did you gain from letting all those men inside you?

Not only are women encouraged to be sluts, they're told their libidos are the same as men's. That's an egregious lie. I found my favorite description of the male sex drive in the book *Letters to My Daughters*, by political consultant Mary Matalin. You know: the one who's married to the bald guy? In the book, she shares an anecdote from her mother, who once said to Mary, "Men would screw a snake if it would sit still long enough."[1]

I know, right? I couldn't stop laughing when I first read it. Don't take it literally—most men aren't that bad. It's just a funny take on what is undoubtedly the biggest difference between men and women. You could never turn that sentence around and say *women* would screw a snake if it would sit still long enough. The visual is preposterous! Sex just isn't a woman's primary M.O.

That doesn't mean women don't *enjoy* sex; they're just not obsessed with it the way men are. According to neuropsychiatrist Louann Brizendine, author of *The Female Brain* and *The Male Brain*, sexual thoughts float through a man's brain every fifty-two seconds, on average, while a woman may think about sex only once a day.[2]

The reason women *appear* to be obsessed with sex is twofold. For one thing, America is saturated with sexual images and messages. To grow up in modern America, you'd think sex is the purpose of our existence. There's no perspective on the subject at all. Women have also been assured that deep down, they really do want to be sluts. Society just didn't allow women to express themselves in this manner until feminism came along to liberate them.

What a load of hooey. Women are literally *made* to bond, and because of this are generally unable to separate sex from emotion. The whole "love 'em and leave 'em" thing just isn't a female practice—which is something that should be honored and respected, not minimized or ridiculed. It used to be. People didn't know *why* women were different from men because the science wasn't there yet, but they knew it just the same. They knew it from experience, and they knew it in their gut.

Today we have proof. The female body, it turns out, is steeped in oxytocin and estrogen, two chemicals that together produce an environment ripe for attachment. Oxytocin, known primarily as the female reproductive hormone, is particularly relevant. Oxytocin causes a woman to bond with the person with whom she's intimately engaged. It also acts as a gauge to help her determine whether or not she should trust the person she's with.

Men have oxytocin, too, but a smaller amount. They're more favored with testosterone—which controls lust, not attachment. That's why *women*, not men, wait by the phone the next day after a one-night stand. That's why the movie *He's Just Not That Into You* wasn't titled *She's Just Not That Into You*. When a woman has sexual contact of any kind, it's an emotional experience, whether she intends it to be or not. The moment touch occurs, oxytocin gets released and the attachment process begins. It just doesn't happen the same way for men. Call it unfair, but there it is.

Let me tell you what I've begun to tell my thirteen-year-old daughter about sex and will continue to tell her, in age-appropriate fashion, as she goes through adolescence: *modesty is what true empowerment is about.* Being restrained, or cautious, with one's sexuality is what it means to be truly empowered. Any woman can strut her stuff and sleep with the hottest guy in town—that's no big feat—but the woman who chooses not to stands out.

Setting high standards for oneself garners not just self-respect but respect from others. There's nothing more attractive than a savvy woman who doesn't become jello in the presence of a hottie. If she likes a guy, she doesn't let him know it. Instead, she holds her cards close to her chest until she determines his intentions and character.

Have you seen *Pride and Prejudice*? The one with Colin Firth? It *must* be the one with Colin Firth. If you haven't, you should. And if you have, watch it again. Study the relationship between Elizabeth and Mr. Darcy, and you'll note the sexual energy that positively drips off the screen. That's what happens when two people don't jump into bed together the moment they meet, or anytime soon afterward. A relationship develops, and the sex comes later. You can rarely reverse these two without it ending in heartache.

I don't say this stuff because I'm a prude. On the contrary, I'm very open about sex. (I can see my friends nodding their heads now!) I think sex is great. *But it has its place.* And that place is absolutely, definitely, not on the first date. Or the second, or third, or even twentieth. Sex—and by that I mean the real thing (thanks to Bill Clinton, we have to be specific)—should occur only within the context of a loving, monogamous relationship with a man who loves and respects you. This takes time to build; and the longer you hold out, the more powerful it will be. If you wait until you're married, even better.

There's no question modern women are more sexually savvy than their grandmothers were. But unlike their grandmothers, they know next to nothing about how to make a relationship work. (Which camp would you rather be in?) That's because women have been taught that gender roles are constricting and that modesty is a form of repression. They represent an archaic social construct designed to hold women down.

That was the engine of the sexual revolution. Prior to the 1970s, Americans understood that men and women are different, not just physically but emotionally. Men honored women's femininity, or even wholesomeness, *not* because they thought women were weaker or "less than" but because (ironically) they believed women were superior!

That may sound odd, but it's true. Women have always been viewed as moral agents, or men's "better half." For years, this was a dominant theme in Hollywood films such as *It's a Wonderful Life* or *The African Queen*. Men *need* women to help steer them in a healthy direction. Without women, men would be content to roam the forest and kill things.

Okay, I'm exaggerating. But still. From the moment males come out of the womb, who's responsible for civilizing them? Women. Women are the arbiters of male conduct. That's why we need women to act like women and not men.

This reminds me of one of my favorite exchanges. It took place in 1972, between journalist Lawrence E. Spivak and feminist icon Gloria Steinem on *Meet the Press*. Spivak said to Steinem, "You made a speech at the National Press Club in which you said, and I quote, 'Women are not taken seriously in this country. We're undervalued, ridiculed, or ignored by a society which consciously or unconsciously assumes the white male is the standard and the norm.' Now, what's your explanation for this serious state of affairs in view of the fact that males are virtually controlled and dominated by women from birth to puberty and often beyond that?"[3]

Steinem was genuinely stumped. Not being a mother herself, all she could say was that she didn't accept the premise of Spivak's statement. In other words, she thought males are *not* dominated by females. Ha. Ask my ten-year-old son, whose teachers are all female and who (in addition to his father) lives with his mother, sister, and grandmother. From the day males are born, their lives are unquestionably dominated by women. Even single-parent homes are predominantly female-headed.

Despite the current dearth of marriageable men, I believe most guys would be more than willing to find a woman with whom they can settle down. But if women don't create an environment that's conducive to this goal, if they offer a smorgasbord of sex and even agree to live with their boyfriends with no commitment, men will delay marriage as long as possible. They just aren't programmed to commit the way women are.

So where does this leave you? Well, there's no question the hook-up culture has made it twice as difficult for women to find husbands. Men may be passing you by and going where they can get some action. That *is* unfortunate. But it's good news, too. It means you can weed out the bad guys to make way for the good guy. Because the guy who wants to continuously get laid isn't the kind of guy you want to marry anyway.

Which brings me back to *Pride and Prejudice*. In the story, Wickham is the bad guy—a player, or nineteenth-century "bad boy." Mr. Darcy, on the other hand, is the good guy—though very proud (and it takes Elizabeth, by the way—a *woman*—to make him less prideful). Nevertheless, Darcy has his pick of any woman he wants. But he's interested only in the woman who pays him the least amount of attention: Elizabeth.

That's because Elizabeth sees through Darcy's conceit and doesn't throw herself at him the way other women do, which makes Darcy all the more hungry for her "affections," as they called it then. Elizabeth wants very much to get married but refuses to marry for money. She wants to marry for love, to a man of character—and it takes her a long time to figure out whether Darcy fits the bill. In the meantime, Elizabeth is patient *and reserved*; and she busies herself with her own life and interests. This makes Darcy fall in love with her all the more.

Whenever I watch *Pride and Prejudice*—or any classic film, for that matter—I think about today's films and television programs, where men and women take off their clothes at the first introduction. I consider how totally devoid of romance and meaning it all is. I reflect on how sad it is that women have been so misled. I think about how women are cavorting around, pretending they want to screw a snake for the sake of pure pleasure, when what they really want, in the end, is someone to love—and someone who'll love them back. What a profound and beautiful gift that is.

And we totally dismiss it.

# 4

# EXPECTATIONS

L ET ME GUESS. All the women in your life—your mother, your professors, your friends, your mentors—expect you to make a career the focus of your life. Marriage was rarely talked about; or if it did come up, it was looked upon as something so far in the future only a fool would spend time thinking about it. Is that about right? The message to modern women is clear: career first, marriage later—much later. Maybe even not at all. If you want to be like everyone else, or heck, just be *normal*, you don't plan your life around being a wife. No one does that.

I'm sorry you can't talk openly to your friends and family about your desire to get married and have a family. But I assure you, your friends who give no thought to marriage now will be running to the altar when their biological clocks start winding down. Modern women have been taught to ignore their biological clocks until the final hour—the assumption being there'll always be a pot of young men willing to go along with this plan.

It rarely works that way. And the women who do find husbands often suffer long, painful, and expensive procedures trying to conceive a child in unorthodox ways, after which they're expected not to savor the result but instead find "quality" child care and continue with life as it was before. What's hopeful about that?

I'm reminded of a woman named Laurie Wagner, whom I wrote about in my first book, *7 Myths of Working Mothers*. She described her view of motherhood this way: "I had it all planned out: I'd birth Ruby, bond with her, and then resume life as I knew it, writing, working, reading, going to movies and restaurants. Ruby would be nearby, strapped on to me like some exotic appendage, delightful, lovely, and obedient, living my life with me. And then, one June, Ruby came."[1]

That's how your generation was taught to map out their lives: as though husbands and children are supposed to accommodate *you*. Scores of women postpone motherhood because they know a baby will curtail their career plans. What no one tells them is how dramatically their lives will change *for the better* once they become mothers. What no one tells women is that this is when their life will in fact begin.

One of the most shocking discoveries is when women realize how much they love their babies and want to be with them. Some years ago I spoke with a woman who had quit her job as a nurse in the Navy to become a full-time mom. Her son was just over a year old at the time, and I asked her what had changed her mind about staying home with him. She said, "I just want to be with him. I got to thinking, 'What's the point of having children in the first place?'"

When I asked her why she hadn't thought she might feel this way beforehand, she said it never occurred to her to *not* go back to work. After all, there was a daycare center right across the street from where she worked, so she assumed everything would work out great. "But," she said, "no one ever told me how much I would miss him."

Women simply change when they have children. Not for the *worse*—for the better. In previous generations, women embraced this transformation and viewed motherhood as the beginning, not the end, of their lives. Today women view it as something to be postponed, something to worry about later, something that gets in the way of their better plans. When my mother attended her graduate school reunion at Radcliffe, one of the female professors gave a lecture about work and family and said women would need to deal with children as an "intrusion" in their lives.

And so it is that women are surprised to find themselves consumed with maternal desire. When they finally do become mothers, many are shocked to discover that what they thought was important before they had children feels utterly irrelevant afterward. This is what marks the change in a woman's value system, a change that becomes more amplified over the years.

In Part Two of this book, I've laid out a twelve-step program designed to challenge the negative messages women like you receive from culture about romance, family, career, and success so you can make the right decisions for your future. Whom you choose to marry is *the most important decision you'll ever make in your lifetime*. It is therefore critical that you approach this decision without the clutter of social expectations.

And of all the expectations of women today, the most significant—and destructive—is the notion that women can have everything they want all at the same time: a great marriage, a fabulous career, and a couple of impressive kiddos.

But as Anne-Marie Slaughter intimated in her wildly successful cover story in *The Atlantic* (July/August 2012), titled, "Why Women Still Can't Have It All," this is a bold-faced lie. Slaughter's article hit a global nerve, for millions of women know the truth about the promises of feminism. "For the remainder of my stint in Washington," wrote Slaughter, "I was increasingly aware that the feminist beliefs in which I had built my entire career were shifting under my feet."[2]

Indeed, feminism didn't teach women how to have it all. It *kept* women from having it all by insisting they focus solely on their careers while ignoring their desire for marriage and motherhood. That's not having it all. That's having half.

Too many people don't realize what feminism did. It didn't just change Americans' understanding of sex and gender roles. *It changed the very meaning of life.* It took the spotlight off the things that matter—love, family, and a sense of place—and put it where it doesn't belong: on money, power, and status. It altered who we are as a people.

At the end of the day, it comes down to this question: What do you want? What do you *value*? Because no matter where you are in life, you can always pull a U-ey and start heading toward what really matters. If what you want is some version of everything—meaningful work, a good marriage, and a healthy dose of motherhood and apple pie—you're in perfectly good company. That's what most women want. And there's no reason you can't have it. But first you have to shift your entire focus.

I know everything I'm writing contradicts what you've been told by the women in your life. And I know it must be difficult to accept that your mentors—perhaps even your own mother—have been, well . . .

I was going to say misguided, but let's call it what it is: wrong.

I'm afraid, however, this is something your generation is going to have to deal with because there's *nothing* empowering about moving in and out of countless romantic relationships, postponing marriage indefinitely, or pursuing careers with a verve that belies common sense. There's nothing empowering about shacking up, rejecting your husband's surname, ignoring your biological clock, refusing to depend on a husband (and thus feeling compelled to return to work after you give birth), or becoming a single mom. To be truly empowered, you're going to have to do a 180.

There's no other way.

*Part Two*

# THE 12-STEP PROGRAM

*"We must learn to think in ways quite unlike the ways feminism taught us to think."*

—Danielle Crittenden

*Step #1*

# LIVE AN EXAMINED LIFE

NOW IT'S TIME TO BEGIN your recovery. I hope you'll be able to enlist your friends in this twelve-step program, but keep in mind it may be a while before they're ready. Some, of course, will never be ready. But you *are*. So grab a glass of wine, put on some cozy socks, and get comfortable. We have a lot to cover.

At the end of the day, people live one of two lives: an examined life, or an unexamined life. It has been my observation that most people choose the latter. An unexamined life is when you move through the years mindlessly, not really thinking about what you're doing or why you're doing it, or even if you *like* doing it. You're just doing it, whatever "it" is, because that's what other people are doing—because that's what you think you're supposed to do. Or because, quite frankly, it's easier. Living an unexamined life means living a life someone else designed *for* you.

The examined life is different. The examined life is when you tune out the voices, sounds, and visuals in your midst and make important decisions based on what *you* want and what *you* believe is right. More than anything, it means dismissing cultural trends that conflict with your core beliefs.

This is extremely hard to do, of course, which is why most people don't do it. But if you want to live an authentic life, it must be done. As Gordon MacDonald wrote in *Ordering Your Private World*, "Few of us can fully appreciate the terrible conspiracy of noise there is about us, noise that denies us the silence and solitude we need for this cultivation of the inner garden."[1]

Most of this "noise" comes in the form of media. Earlier generations were fortunate: they lived primarily with their own thoughts and the views of their friends and family. We do not. Instead, the "conspiracy of noise" we endure 24/7 clouds our vision and impairs our judgment, pulling us away from our own beliefs and desires. Simply put, we no longer think for ourselves.

The only way to live an examined life is to avoid the chatter in your midst. This includes *any* media that sends messages that are counterproductive to your goal. And if you've picked up this book, we both know your goal is to get—and, presumably, stay—married, which means there's going to be a helluva a lot of media you're going to have to ignore.

There's more. Once you remove these negative cultural messages (and I realize you can't do this 100 percent), to ensure you don't get sucked back in, you'll need to distance yourself from friends who don't do likewise. That will be especially hard. But if you want to make the right decision about whom, when, and under what circumstances to marry, it must be done.

I cannot stress the power of trends enough. Some trends are benign— like big hair in the 1980s—but some, such as promiscuity, are not. Either way, the trend becomes absorbed in the culture to such a degree that people feel compelled to jump on board, even if they'd rather not. Like I said, it's just easier and more comfortable to go along with the crowd. That isn't *always* a bad thing, but it can be. Depends what the crowd is doing.

When it comes to making good decisions in life, particularly big ones, it is *absolutely essential* that you surround yourself with positive influences. The more you surround yourself with people or messages that support your goal, the more successful you will be in your mission. It really is the whole enchilada.

As an example, suppose you wanted to lose a bunch of weight and had a choice between two doors you could open to help you accomplish your goal. Behind the first door is a roomful of obese people, and behind the second door is a roomful of strong, healthy, fit people—Dr. Oz types. Which door would you want to open? It's a no-brainer, isn't it? If you're serious about losing weight, you need to be around people who can help you get there. The same is true with marriage.

To drive this point home, let's assume you weren't born when you were. Let's say you were born in the 1940s instead, when divorce was uncommon and when there was no such thing as the Internet. In this case, the influences in your life would be mainly friends and family—the people you'd see and hear from the most. Now, let's also assume your parents were one of the few couples you knew who happened to be divorced. How might your beliefs about marriage be different?

You'd no doubt be skeptical, given your role models. Only you would have an advantage because most of the rest of your family members—your aunts, uncles, cousins, etc.—*would* be married, as would your friends and neighbors, thus providing you with a different model from the one you have at home. And since television and the Internet don't exist, you wouldn't be walloped every day with headlines and slogans that tell you this woman's getting a divorce or that woman's become a single mother by choice. Nor would you be exposed to programs like *Sex and the City* that promote promiscuity, materialism, and a "You Go, Girl" attitude. Instead, most of what you would see would be families that consist of married parents and their children.

It cannot be overstated: the environment in which we are raised is critical. People are heavily influenced by what they see and hear around them. Whatever support and camaraderie we experience will significantly affect, for better or for worse, the decisions we make.

But alas, you were not born in the 1940s. In the world you know, divorce is rampant, and telecommunications is a way of life. That means you're privy to what everyone else is doing, or what it *looks* like everyone else is doing. That perception—and 99 percent of the time it's just that: a perception—is that women everywhere are living carefree lives devoid of any responsibility. Other than their jobs, of course, and those are touted as glamorous, not laborious. This perception makes the average woman feel insecure about the kind of life she wants to build for herself. All of a sudden, getting married and having babies seems so . . . irrelevant. Stupid, even.

And here's the worst part: the lives of the women we see in the media aren't even real. It's all an illusion. Which means everyday women are making very real decisions about their very real lives based on something they absorb as real but isn't!

As a consumer of media, you're not supposed to be a passive observer when you watch those romantic comedies or read about the lives of Hollywood starlets. You're not supposed to just *watch* the Katie Courics of the world, or the women on *The View*, or even Giada De Laurentiis on Food Network. You're supposed to *identify* with these women.

This wouldn't be a problem if the women in the media represented, or even *touted*, the values most Americans share. But they don't. Most of the high-profile women we hear from on a regular basis are single, divorced, lesbian, or hard-core working mothers with well-paid nannies. And these women, along with their colleagues, are responsible for framing the cultural debate. Here are just a few headlines of the past few years:

"Who Needs Marriage?" (*Time*, Nov. 18, 2010)

"The End of Men "(*The Atlantic*, July/Aug 2010)

"For Women, Is Home Really So Sweet?" (*The Wall Street Journal*, Feb. 18, 2012)

"Is It Time to Retire the Word 'Wife'"? (*The Huffington Post*, Feb. 15, 2012)

"Do You Hate Your Husband?" (*Yahoo*, Dec. 5, 2010)

"Stay-at-home moms more depressed than working moms, study finds" (*Today Show*, May 18, 2012)

Headlines like these are commonplace. They are *the norm*. (And by the way, can you even imagine a headline that read, "Do You Hate Your Wife?" The double standard is astounding.) But if you'd been born in the 1940s, it would never occur to you to think along these lines. You wouldn't be skeptical of men in general, nor would you assume marriage is suffocating. Instead, the messages you'd receive from society, *despite your parents' example*, would be positive. Helpful. They would be pro-marriage and pro-family.

Unfortunately, you were born at a time when fractured families are the rule, not the exception. Almost everyone you know has either been divorced or has been affected by divorce. Moreover, your source of support and camaraderie is no longer family and community—it's the media. Strangers. Women with whom you have nothing in common.

Which brings us to the million-dollar question: How are you going to block out this "terrible conspiracy of noise"?[2] Are you going to live intentionally? Or mindlessly?

As I see it, you have two options. You can absorb the messages and make decisions based on what the prevailing culture tells you is the 'thing to do' (and thus live an unexamined life). Or, you can tune out what you see and hear around you and go with your gut. Because the fact is, if you regularly absorb pop culture—and by that I mean mainstream news media, television sitcoms and dramas, women's magazines, and Hollywood films—your views on marriage are being heavily influenced by all the wrong people.

Your friends will deny this vociferously. "Oh, I watch and read that stuff," they'll say, "but it doesn't affect me." I'm sure they believe this, but it's naïve. Here's an idea: try turning off modern-day TV shows for a week and watching black-and-white films instead. Or better yet, read a romance novel from the early twentieth century. Afterward, see if the way you look at love isn't different. I'd be shocked if it isn't. The folks who produce the material that gets delivered to your doorstep every day—via television, magazines, and the Internet—depend on your absorbing their messages. These folks are in business because women like you consume the material.

Lest you think I'm exaggerating, former editor of *Ladies' Home Journal* Myrna Blyth exposed these folks in *Spin Sisters*: "Spin sisters are members of the female media elite, a Girls' Club of editors, producers, and print and television journalists with similar attitudes and opinions who influence the way millions of American women think and feel about their lives, their world, and themselves."[3] And what are the spin sisters selling? The absurd notion that American women are unduly burdened, that they have the cards stacked against them, and that they're ultimately better off without men.

Indeed, modern women's views on men and marriage have been filtered through a feminist lens, rather than through the lens of everyday Americans who have your best interests at heart. The women of your generation don't stand a chance of being happily married unless they *disregard the cultural messages they're besieged with every day*. The women in most of the media may know a great deal about how to read a teleprompter, but their personal lives are a mess. They're the last people on earth who should be dispensing advice about marriage and motherhood.

Now, I wish I could say that's all there is to it. Unfortunately, even if you steer clear of pop culture, many of your friends will not—which means they'll have a different take on how things should be. As a result, your friends may try to steer you in a direction you don't want to go. That's why trends are so powerful: even if *you* reject them, they affect you indirectly via your friends. And rejecting your friends, or at least their advice and opinions, is significantly harder than rejecting the media.

To say trends are powerful isn't enough. They're wicked. We humans suffer constant turmoil over what we believe is the right thing to do versus what we know is the popular thing to do. It begins when we're young and never lets up—adults are just as bad as kids. I know plenty of people who compare themselves to their neighbors incessantly, not necessarily because they want to be better but because they want to fit in. They want to belong, even at the expense of doing what's best for themselves and their families.

*Don't let this be your fate.* Stop caring right now, today, about what other people think and do—whether it's the women in the media or the woman next door. If you want to make choices commensurate with what *you* want as opposed to what other people say you should want, you have no other choice.

Deep down, most women want to have a traditional family; they're just too afraid to admit it. They think the desire to be a wife and mother means being less than what a woman can, or should, be. As writer/producer Dani Klein Modisett admitted in an article entitled "My Kids Stole My Ambition!" being employed was how she "justified her existence."[4] Ms. Modisett is not alone. Many, many women feel this way, and it makes perfect sense given the environment in which they were raised.

Don't pay attention to a culture that values money over love. Instead, listen to your gut. Live an examined life. As the late Steve Jobs once said, "Your time is limited, so don't waste it living someone else's life. Don't be trapped by dogma—which is living with the results of other people's thinking. Don't let the noise of others' opinions drown out your own inner voice. Have the courage to follow your heart and intuition. They somehow already know what you truly want to become."[5]

*Step #2*

# GET OVER YOURSELF

S TEP #2 OF YOUR DETOX is sort of an extension of Step #1—it has to do with your friends. You know, the ones who told you you're crazy for even *thinking* about marriage until you've "found yourself." The notion that women should 'find themselves' has been around since I was your age and has become even more pronounced over the years. The idea is that a woman must first become the person she's supposed to become. Then—and only then—should she entertain the idea of becoming someone's wife or mother.

Allow me to begin at the end: this is rubbish.

It's a lovely notion, the idea of finding oneself. In fact, theoretically I like it. And I get the point: rather than women going from daddy to hubby, the way they did in the old days, they should spend time alone, getting to know who they are, before tethering themselves to a man.

It's not that I don't think women (and men, for that matter) should live on their own and figure out what they want before getting married—I do. It's the concept of "finding oneself" that disturbs me. Very few people, male or female, "find" themselves in their twenties or even thirties. It takes *decades* to figure out who we are and what we're capable of. I'm forty-five and just now getting it.

The late Julia Child felt the same way. "I was thirty-seven years old and still discovering who I was."[1] This is the process of maturation, and it usually happens as a result of living a very long time and having many different experiences, the most significant of which is marriage.

Think about it. How can you know who you really are until you learn how to react in difficult, challenging situations where you're forced to sacrifice, look inward, and make necessary adjustments for personal growth? One of my favorite quotes that I keep close by is by preacher Chuck Swindoll, who said, "Life is 10 percent what happens to you and 90 percent how you react to it."[2] It takes years to cultivate one's identity, and marriage and motherhood help this along.

People's priorities change when they get married. When you're single, life outside of work is largely without obligations or sacrifice. When you're married with children, you learn the art of compromise and unconditional love. *That's* when you "find yourself." A woman named Ariana Jalfen left a great comment online in an article about marriage. She said, "Growth hand-in-hand with a like-minded person is the point—not growth in order to meet a like-minded person. Unless the goal is to marry a mirror image of yourself (with a penis), there's no need to become the person you want to attract."

So, living on one's own before getting married (as opposed to jumping from Mom and Dad to a husband or wife) is important, yes, but *not* because by twenty-eight you'll have discovered who you are. It's important because people learn to be self-sufficient. Specifically, women learn how to support themselves, and men learn how to be domestic.

These are great tools, even if each of these duties falls primarily on one spouse's shoulders once people settle down to family life. I would never suggest, for example, that a woman not get an education because she plans to devote her life to family. None of us can predict the way our lives will unfold—we should all be prepared for the unforeseen.

The problem with the "finding oneself" argument is that the years of living solo tend to drag on, which brings me to the second problem with the concept. Somewhere along the line, the stated goal got lost in the shuffle. In *The Paradox of Choice*, Barry Schwartz wrote, "Whereas delaying marriage and avoiding commitment would seem to promote self-discovery, this freedom and self-exploration seems to leave many people feeling more lost than found."[3]

Makes sense, doesn't it? It's not as though your single friends have embarked on some sort of spiritual meditation. They probably spend their days going to the office, hitting the bars, watching TV, and having sex. Many stay in school for upwards of a decade or longer, either bleeding their parents dry or racking up serious debt. Most women don't spend ten or fifteen years in some sort of perfect self-exploration and then say, "Okay, I'm ready to get married now!" only to have Mr. Right waiting patiently on the sidelines—whereupon the two ride off into the sunset. On the contrary, one of three things usually occurs:

1.   The woman gets bored trying to find herself or realizes her clock is ticking, at which point she decides she'd better hurry up and get married. Only trouble is, she can't find a willing participant.

2.   The woman finds a willing participant but realizes sometime later that she chose him out of convenience and that he wasn't the right choice of husband after all.

3.   The woman marries her longtime lover but suffers a huge emotional and financial toll trying to conceive even one child, let alone two.

Rachel Lehmann-Haupt is one such woman. In an article entitled "The Aniston Syndrome," she wrote that just before her thirty-seventh (thirty-*seventh*!) birthday, she told the man she loved that she was ready to settle down and have a child. "I've had all this freedom to come this far in my career, and I've finally found myself, and as a result I found you," she told him. "Now I have no control over my biology."[4]

But her guy didn't want to get married. And of her "waning fertility," he callously responded, "It's nature's cruel joke on women."[5]

Lehmann-Haupt has it all wrong. She didn't find the love of her life as a result of finding herself. She's just repeating the script she was sold. Like so many women of her generation, Lehmann-Haupt was focused exclusively on herself and her career, and thought Mr. Right would magically appear according to her own timetable. She was then willing to settle for the man she happened to be with at the time. "If I could go back ten years," she says, "I would tell my younger self that she should deeply consider her future family . . . I wonder whether in fact my generation collectively screwed up."[6]

What women like Lehmann-Haupt learned the hard way is that delaying marriage indefinitely in order to find oneself really just translates to "pursuing advanced degrees, establishing oneself in the workforce, and living day to day." And that course of action, over too long a time, is counterproductive to settling down with a husband and kids.

Now if marriage and motherhood are not the goal, fine. More power to you. Take Kathryn Kelly, who was featured in *The Wall Street Journal*. When Ms. Kelly was young, her goal was to become a chef. She ended up drifting from that goal and instead got multiple degrees in public health and worked for years in the corporate sector. After she tired of that, she decided to pursue her lifelong dream and enroll in culinary school.

Two years after graduation, Kelly was offered a job at Oceania Cruises as a chef. Today, she spends ten months at sea and "has to stop and pinch herself" every now and then when she realizes she's an actual chef who gets to lead onshore excursions to markets and restaurants in places like Sicily, where she learned to "make cannoli and tasted lava-grown wine on Mount Etna."[7]

Ms. Kelly's life sounds glamorous, doesn't it? Very cool, indeed. But in order for her to live the life she's chosen, she had to forgo having a traditional family. (The story did mention a daughter Kelly "raised on her own" somewhere along the way, but no other details were given.) Few people can pursue this kind of life if marriage and motherhood are the goal. Something's got to give.

The concept of finding oneself originated around the time of the sexual revolution. By the time you and your friends were born, America had fully embraced the New Age philosophy that baby boomers set forth more than forty years ago. Before the 1960s, Americans hadn't heard of this notion. They were too busy dealing with the realities of life to engage in such an existential crisis. That was a boomer thing.

People also weren't focused on the self. Prior to the 1960s, Americans embraced a universal moral order. This was a philosophy that focused on the health and well-being of *everyone*, not just the needs and desires of the individual. This moral order wasn't necessarily a religious order (though that was part of it); it was more of an understanding that as citizens of a large community, we have a moral obligation to do the right thing and take into account how our choices affect those around us. Americans, for

HOW TO CHOOSE A HUSBAND

the most part, agreed on right and wrong, believed in God, and viewed family as society's great stabilizer.

But several factions emerged in the 1960s—the antiwar activists and supporters of the feminist movement, for example—to turn this moral order on its head. Rather than expecting people to obey God or subscribe to a universal concept of right and wrong, these groups argued that people should focus on what's best for them as individuals. Boomers loved this idea since they were all about doing what feels good rather than doing what's right. (It was a time of great rebellion, as I'm sure you've heard.) Before long, voilà: the idea of being "true to oneself" was born.

This New Age philosophy still exists today and has officially replaced the universal moral order to which Americans once adhered. Religion is no longer a unifying force. Rather, we are mired in moral relativism; that is, the freedom to do what we want, when we want, with no judgment or interference from society. To many people, moral relativism *is* a religion.

Referring to life in the '60s, Charles Murray wrote, "To accept the concept of virtue requires that you believe some ways of behaving are right and others are wrong always and everywhere. That openly judgmental stand is no longer acceptable in America's schools, nor in many American homes."[8] Indeed. That's because moral relativism wiped it out.

But this selfish approach to life—doing what you want, when you want—rarely produces the desired result, particularly when it comes to family. Instead it fosters a life that becomes so self-serving that when women eventually do get married—if they can find a man who's willing to marry them—it becomes difficult, if not impossible, to shift gears and take into account other individuals who have needs and desires of their own.

Moral relativism is a black stain on American culture. It bloomed and blossomed to the point where it now holds people back from their true potential as human beings—as women, as friends, as wives, as mothers. Those who came of age after the 1960s have no frame of reference for thinking or acting selflessly. They've been taught that the needs of the individual should always take precedence.

The current generation has it even worse: they've been taught to believe they're so special life should be handed to them on a silver platter. Perfection is the goal—they *deserve* it. But anyone who tells you you're entitled to perfection has done you a great disservice.

Have you heard the commencement speech from Dr. David McCullough of Wellesley High School, including his now infamous proclamation, "You're Not Special"? His point is that people have been so "pampered, cosseted, doted upon . . . feted and fawned over and called sweetie pie" that they've lost the understanding—and benefit—of what it means to work hard, sacrifice, and commit to something:

> You are not exceptional.
>
> Contrary to what your U9 soccer trophy suggests, your glowing seventh grade report card, despite every assurance of a certain corpulent purple dinosaur, that nice Mr. Rogers and your batty Aunt Sylvia, no matter how often your maternal caped crusader has swooped in to save you, you are nothing special . . .
>
> . . . The fulfilled life is a consequence, a gratifying byproduct. It's what happens when you're thinking about more important things. Climb the mountain not to plant your flag, but to embrace the challenge, enjoy the air and behold the view. Climb it so you can see the world, not so the world can see you. Go to Paris to be in Paris, not to cross it off your list and congratulate yourself for being worldly. Exercise free will and creative, independent thought not for the satisfactions they will bring you, but for the good they will do others, the rest of the 6.8 billion—and those who will follow them. And then you too will discover the great and curious truth of the human experience is that selflessness is the best thing you can do for yourself.[9]

*No other role* in your life will require more selflessness than being a wife and mother. If you want to be successful at it, you need to start thinking about other people's needs. You need to ignore all that coddling you've been given and stop thinking in terms of what you think you deserve or are entitled to. To have a fulfilling, beautiful life—the best life you can have—you don't need to *find* yourself.

You need to get over yourself.

So...back to those friends of yours who think you shouldn't get married until you've "found" yourself and who've begged you not to "settle" for anything less than you deserve. Ignore them.

In ten years, they'll be miserable—and you won't.

*Step #3*

# RETURN TO FEMININITY

Y OU KNOW THOSE WOMEN who have it all together professionally but can't for the life of them get their love lives in order? There's actually a phrase for these ladies: "smart in life, dumb in love." I read an article recently by a woman named Kris Fuchs who said, "My business runs just fine. It's my personal life I find so difficult."[1] For many women today, this is par for the course.

Highly educated, professional women—and by that I don't mean women with college degrees; I mean women with degree upon degree or women with high-profile careers—used to be a rare breed, but today they're commonplace. It's no coincidence, however, that at the same time women have "risen" in the marketplace, marriage has taken a nosedive. Power and love are hopelessly at odds. If you want to find love, you need to stop being in charge all the time and learn how to embrace your femininity. If you do, you'll find a different kind of power awaits you.

As men can attest, women struggle with this. They're so focused on outward achievement, they can't get in touch with their softer side. They suffocate their feminine tendencies in order to prove something to themselves and the world. Remember Rachel Fine? The woman who said, "I've always thrived in a man's world, and to do that, you almost have to shut off your girlie side"? That's exactly what I mean.

Why should we be surprised that women feel they need to shut off their girlie side? Since the day they were born, they've been encouraged to ignore their hardwiring. Women have been conditioned to believe they live in an unequal world where the cards are stacked against them—and that to rectify this so-called problem, they should chuck their feminine proclivities and adopt male traits and behaviors.

Enough already.

"Male and female brains are different from the moment of conception," wrote neuropsychiatrist Louann Brizendine. "There are deep differences, at the level of every cell, between the male and female brain. A male cell has a Y chromosome and the female does not. That small but significant difference begins to play out early in the brain as genes set the stage for later amplification by hormones."[2]

As an example, Brizendine describes one of her patients who gave her toddler daughter a handful of unisex toys, including a bright red fire truck. "She walked into her daughter's room one afternoon to find her cuddling the truck in a baby blanket, rocking it back and forth saying, 'Don't worry, little truckie, everything will be all right.'"[3]

There's nothing unusual about this scenario—it's typical, everyday stuff. But women have become so far removed from their natural tendencies, they no longer recognize they have them. When was the last time you saw a wife or girlfriend be kind and nurturing to her husband or boyfriend? When was the last time you saw her let him hold the door open for her? Or pay the bill? Or look at him when he talks as though he has something important to say? These are old-fashioned feminine habits, and they still work.

The other night I was on a date with my husband, and the woman next to us was berating her husband the entire time. Neither my husband nor I said anything until we got in the car. We were so horrified we decided they must be brother and sister because it was too painful to think their relationship was real. It was . . . ugly. That's the only word I can use to describe it.

Too many women today are ugly. Mean. Gruff. Bitchy. Women like this have been around for centuries, but it wasn't commonplace, the way it is today. Before the sexual revolution, men were respected members of society. They had a role to play, and it was an important one. Women *liked* men and sought them out. "Landing" a husband was considered a coup.

Then women came to view men as oppressors and felt the need to prove themselves equal to any man. And men, generally speaking, aren't soft and sweet. They're rough. Hard. Competitive. So now women are too. "Feminism is central to the state of love today because it rejects the complementary character of men and women—an idea that is central to our cultural tradition. As different as we are, we need one another, and any theory that does not understand that pattern will be destructive," wrote Kenneth Minogue in *The Wall Street Journal*.[4]

And it has been. Feminists want you to believe biology is adaptable, not determinative. They want you to think gender shouldn't dictate or limit anyone's choice. Men can do what women do just as well as women, and women can do what men do just as well as men. Not only *can* they, deep down they want to. The only reason there aren't more female fire-fighters and more male preschool teachers is because parents and society raise the sexes to think a certain way—you know: by giving girls dolls and boys trucks, that sort of thing.

Feminists have been so successful preaching this myth (even though the most outspoken among them don't have children and thus have no idea what they're talking about) that your generation grew up believing males and females have the same goals, desires, and abilities. Should you run into any disparities in this regard—and you will—it's not due to biology. They simply prove we live in a patriarchy. The "patriarchy" is the reason women "still" make less than men. It's why there aren't more female CEOs, and it's why the vast majority of stay-at-home parents are women.

But this radical concept of gender is new. It may be all *you* know, but you're not that old. Most Americans didn't grow up with this mythical view of male and female nature. It has always been understood that men bring something to the table that women don't, and vice versa. But after decades of feminist propaganda, Americans have come to believe otherwise. Some women don't believe men bring anything to the table at all, except maybe sperm.

I know it's painful to listen to your friends talk about men in such a disparaging manner. And yet, isn't it interesting they still want to get married? Sadly, they're going to struggle to find (and keep) husbands—for two reasons. One, they have their dukes up. That's not a relationship; that's a fight. Two, they don't understand men—and thus don't appreciate the male/female dance. *What it takes to get a man into bed is not the same as what it takes to get a man to the altar.* Your generation desperately needs an education about relationship dynamics.

So let's get started.

A long, long time ago, people didn't know why men and women were different, but intuition and common sense told them what they needed to know: males and females are not the same. Since your generation has come to believe equality means sameness, in order to believe the sexes really are different, you need proof.

Fortunately, we have it. The research on brain differences has exploded over the past decade—it's all there in black and white. For instance, did you know the female brain secretes more serotonin than the male brain? Serotonin is important because it relates directly to impulse control. Men are far more likely to drink and drive, for example. They're also more prone to suicide.

And sex? As we already learned, sex takes up a lot of space in the male brain. The best illustration I can offer about the difference between men and women when it comes to sex is this: How many men do you know who'd be offended if a woman told him she'd like to use his body for sex? Now turn that scenario around. If a man told a woman he'd like to use her body for sex, it would be grounds for sexual harassment. Apples and oranges.

And remember when we talked about oxytocin, the chemical that keeps women from being able to have sex without strings attached? Oxytocin isn't just relevant to sex; it's also the reason girls like to play with "care objects." It's why my daughter would find any inanimate object when she was little and pretend it was a baby so she could cradle it, rock it to sleep, and change its diaper.

Males, on the other hand, secrete a lot of serotonin. That particular neurotransmitter is the reason my son would find any inanimate object when he was little and pretend it had the power to kill. Parents don't *teach* their little girls to be "into" babies (or weddings, for that matter), nor do they *teach* their little boys to be "into" guns, as society suggests. These desires are hardwired.

I suspect serotonin is also the reason males love to—and I hate this word—fart. If I had a dollar for every time my son purposefully farted as loud as he could, followed by fits of laughter, I'd be rich. I've heard my daughter pass gas maybe five times in her life. (Notice the delicate switch of terms there . . . ) Only in her case, it was something to be embarrassed about—not something one uses to entertain people.

Females also have an accelerated occipital lobe. This allows their brains to take in more sensory data than boys—which, if you think about the way men and women communicate, makes perfect sense. Women love to analyze things to death, whereas men just want the final conclusion of all that rumination. How many times has a guy asked you to get to the point? Oy vey, I'm embarrassed to answer that one . . .

Finally, there's a part of the brain called the hippocampus. Its main job is memory storage, and it is much larger in females than it is in males. Michael Gurian wrote about this in his books *The Wonder of Girls* and *The Wonder of Boys*. He used an example of a young boy and a young girl being asked by their parents to do three things around the house: clean up their rooms, take out the garbage, and wipe the table. He said that more often than not, we will see the young girl complete the tasks with less reminding than the boy would need and that this has a lot to do with the hippocampal memory. Men are linear in their thinking. Generally speaking, they can focus only on one thing at a time.

Does this sound spurious? If so, that's because you've been conditioned to believe the reason women do more housework and child care is because their chauvinistic husbands expect them to—and that unless men start pulling their weight at home, women will never achieve equality. But most men don't *expect* women to do all the work at home. They just *don't care* whether or not the laundry gets done or the beds get made. My husband's idea of dusting is to wipe a surface clean with the sweep of his arm. Hellooo?

Now, I'm not suggesting that because men don't care as much about these things, you should do all the work yourself. I'm saying that recognizing your husband operates differently than you do will go a long way toward creating peace at home.

That the sexes aren't the same, or "equal" in the way we think they are, has no bearing on the worth of each gender or what each contributes to society as a whole. Your perception of equality is just skewed. Men and women are equal but different. They do not have the same bodies; they do not speak the same language; they do not want the same things; and they do not operate with the same set of tools. Men are men, and women are women. It stands to reason, then, that acting as if male and female are one and the same hinders us rather than helps us.

But make any reference to the differences between the sexes and the feminist media go ballistic. They'll tell you people like me are throwbacks who think the sexes each have their "place," and we should therefore adhere to strict gender roles. Perhaps some people do believe that, but I am not one of them. And quite frankly, I don't know anyone who is. Every couple I know has some crossover with respect to gender roles, myself included. But that doesn't mean we reject the fact that men and women are different, or that we think society's to blame for these differences. Nor does it mean we think men and women should be equally represented in all spheres of life in order to prove some false notion of equality. That's absurd.

The best example of male and female nature I've seen was depicted in *My Big Fat Greek Wedding*. Did you see it? The daughter, Toula, is upset because she can't get her very traditional Greek father to understand that she wants more out of life than just being a wife, so her mother steps in to teach her daughter how women use certain strategies when dealing with men. "Let me tell you something, Toula. The man is the head [of the household], but the woman is the neck. And she can turn the head *any way* she wants."[5]

Modern women have no appreciation for the power wives yield on the home front. The average husband *wants* to please his wife. He *wants* her to be happy and will do anything in his power to make it happen. "To us," wrote comedian Steve Harvey in *Act Like a Lady, Think Like a Man*, "your power comes from one simple thing: you're a woman, and we men will do anything humanly possible to impress you so we can be with you. You're the ultimate prize for us."[6] Meanwhile, all men want in exchange is respect, kindness, and sex.

There isn't much more to it than that.

Unfortunately, these things have all taken a backseat in marriage. Modern American women *do not* respect men. If you have any doubt about this, simply turn on any sitcom and it'll be clear as day. Wives talk to their husbands (and women talk about men) as if they're idiots. I've personally witnessed wives be openly dismissive and disrespectful toward their husbands. They roll their eyes, mock their husbands' salaries, or freely admit to not sleeping with them. These women may as well put a dagger in their husbands' hearts and twist it around and around.

The saddest part is, these wives don't realize they're destroying their marriages. Why would they? Their behavior is not only encouraged, it's mirrored by the women they see around them, both in their neighborhood and in the media. They have no reason to think they're doing anything wrong.

I'm convinced our grandmothers would be shocked if they knew the extent of what goes on in marriages today. But of course our grandmothers were never saddled with such high expectations of marriage. Plus, they respected men and knew sex was part of the deal. They accepted matrimony as a contract.

I imagine that sounds bizarre to you, maybe even gross. Women today prefer to think of marriage as a romantic venture, so *duty* and *obligation* are unfamiliar terms. In fact, the idea of being lawfully required to sleep with someone, even if it is one's spouse, sounds nuts. Many wives joke that their husbands should be grateful for anything they get.

But wives *do* have a duty to sleep with their husbands, just as men have a duty to sleep with their wives. Sex is the glue that holds a marriage together. And men are just wild about it. To get inside the mind of a man, I decided to ask Sam Botta, a celebrity interviewer in Los Angeles, to explain what men want.

Sam is forty-two and divorced (no kids), and he has a super body he works hard to maintain. Having joined eHarmony years ago, he has read thousands of profiles and has had countless first dates. He seems to have a good handle on what women want but says women don't understand what men need. Here's what he told me:

> Sex is a man's only emotional connection—it's like a woman's desire for communication. Men don't like to communicate through lengthy discussions; that's why they always ask women to get to the point.
>
> A woman's primary M.O.—communication—is rarely pleasurable for men. Yet a man's primary M.O.—sex—is very pleasurable for women. So when a man asks his wife for sex, he's not asking her to do something that's not pleasurable, or something that only benefits him. He loves bringing pleasure to his wife. It's how he communicates his love for her.

You can't turn this around. Oftentimes a man likes to have no communication at all—yet if he doesn't spend hours listening to his wife
or girlfriend talk about her feelings or problems, he's considered a
prick. Why, then, should women be allowed to say no to sex whenever
it suits them? That would be like a man cutting off all communication
with his wife or girlfriend when it doesn't suit him. It would be like a
husband saying this to his wife: "Listen, honey, in marriage sometimes
things happen—people close to us become ill, or die, or one of us
gets depressed, etc.—so I think it's reasonable when I don't feel like
talking, listening, or paying any attention to you. I just don't feel like
communicating. Thanks for understanding—just like you expect me
to understand the no-sex thing."[7]

Sam also added that most of the profiles he receives are from women
who present themselves as powerful and independent, as though these
are salable traits. But men aren't impressed with that, he says. What men
want more than anything else in the world is to be respected and admired,
loved and accepted. The rest is largely immaterial.

Sam's comments about sex are eerily similar to those of Steve Harvey,
who referred to sex as "the cookie" in *Act Like a Lady*. "Please—puh-
leeze—don't hold out on the cookie," he wrote. "We don't care about
anything else; we need the cookie. The emotional stuff—the talking, the
cuddling, the holding hands, and bonding, that's y'all's thing. We'll do
those things because we know it's important to you. But please understand: the way we men connect is by having sex. Period."[8]

These differences we're talking about between males and females
start early, by the way. They're visible at birth and become even more
pronounced in grade school. As a former teacher and the mother of a
boy and a girl, I can personally attest to boys' need to move their bodies
or just *do something* active, and girls' preference for sedentary activities
that require being verbal.

As a small example, some months ago my daughter had four friends
sleep over for her birthday. What did they do? Talked. The entire time.
For hours. And the next morning they played "Truth or Dare?" How
many boys do you know who (a) have sleepovers, (b) talk all night, and
(c) play "Truth or Dare?" in the morning? Honestly, I could fill an entire
book with examples of differences between males and females.

What women need to understand is that *the faux version of equality they've been taught undermines love.* Men are hunters. They want to build things and kill things—that's why more men than women shoot guns. It's why male engineers greatly outnumber female engineers. Females, on the other hand, like to gather and nest—that's why more women than men like to shop and bake, or stay home with their kids. Women also like to get all dressed up and prance about in their heels. And men love to *watch* women prance about in their heels. That's the yin and yang of gender relations.

Unfortunately, modern women have lost sight of this fact, or perhaps never understood it in the first place. They were told power comes in the form of money and prestige, not femininity. By changing direction, by turning their attention away from the home and onto the marketplace, women lost the power they once had on the home front. Women have always had the upper hand in marriage. That whole business about husbands oppressing their wives? More often than not, that's feminist gobbledygook. America isn't Iran.

Remember when I said that what it takes to get a man into bed is not the same as what it takes to get a man to the altar? Harvey explained this concept in a chapter titled "Sports Fish vs. Keepers." Men, he wrote, fish for women. But they can only catch what they're able to reel in. "Men will treat women like one of two things: a sports fish or a keeper. A sports fish doesn't have any rules, requirements, respect for herself, or guidelines; and we men can pick up her scent a mile away. She's the party girl." He added, "As soon as she lets a man know he can treat her just any old kind of way, he will do just that."

A keeper, on the other hand, "never gives in easily," he continued. Her high standards and expectations are evident from the get-go. A keeper "understands her power and wields it like a samurai sword. She commands—not demands—respect, just by the way she carries herself." And here's my favorite part of Harvey's analysis: "Men automatically know *from the moment she opens her mouth* [emphasis mine] that if they want her, they'll have to get in line with her standards and requirements."[9]

This psychological seesaw, which has been played out between men and women for centuries, has been eradicated by a society that pushes a unisex agenda. Women have no idea how to use their femininity to their advantage, so they end up rearing their heads, trying to be something they're not. Instead of becoming wives, they become competitors. This is the number one mistake women make.

Let human nature do its thing. Men like to chase women, and women like to be chased—that's just the way it is. Don't become the hunter. Don't call a guy or make the first move. Don't try to take charge or be in control. That's what men are supposed to do. Let them.

A woman's femininity is unique and powerful. It does not lower a woman's status, nor does it preclude her from being an independent woman. In fact, many men prefer their wives *are* independent. So, go. Do what you want with your life—no one's stopping you. Just don't try to compete with your husband. He doesn't want a competitor; he has plenty of those. At the end of the day, what a man wants is a partner and companion who's concerned with his needs as much as her own, maybe even more.

That's what love is.

If you can find a way to tap into your femininity without feeling victimized, you will find the love you so desperately seek. Our post-feminist culture is fighting a gender war that I can assure you has no winner. My advice to you is: stay out of it.

*Step #4*

# DON'T RELY ON LOVE

I'M SURE YOU KNOW THIS ALREADY, at least theoretically, but I must belabor it: Everything that comes out of Hollywood, from conception to delivery, is an illusion. A lie. A fabrication. False. Fake. A mirage. Hollywood is one giant temptation to get you to screw up your life in every conceivable way.

That's why I spent so much time in Step #1 trying to explain the significance—no, the *necessity*—of rejecting pop culture. Because that's what Hollywood is: pop culture. It doesn't matter whether we're talking about movies, television, or even the music you listen to. It all emanates from the same place, and today almost all of it is toxic.

Now, if you're *not* looking for lasting love, by all means zone out in fairy tale land. Have a party. But if you're looking for a *real* life with a *real* man, you're going to have to reject Hollywood. Hollywood *needs* you to believe in fairy tales. It depends on your absorbing its messages and coming back for more. Women inhale "rom-coms" and music with lyrics about love because they desperately want to believe in happily ever after.

It doesn't exist.

Now stay with me here—I don't mean there's no happy ending. I mean the *image* you have of happily ever after does not in any way, shape, or form match the reality. The real happily ever after is 100 percent different from what you imagine. The girl and the guy don't walk off into the sunset together. Well, they do—but the sun will set on some very hard times. Hollywood skips over that part.

To have a marriage that lasts—and please read this over and over again because I literally can't emphasize it enough—*you cannot rely on love*. I know that seems counterintuitive, but there it is. You've heard the phrase "Love doesn't pay the bills." What that means is two people who intend to be married for a lifetime need much more than love to keep them going.

Much more.

A great illustration of how screwed up our priorities are is how women now spend all their time focusing on their wedding day and virtually no time focusing on the marriage itself. They have it all backwards. Weddings are irrelevant in the grand scheme of things. Except for the vows, it's all fluff. Meaningless. Modern weddings represent the party marriage has become.

Marriage is not a party; it's a vocation. After the wedding and honeymoon are over and several years have passed, life settles in—and if a couple got married mainly because they had warm and gooey feelings for each other, or because they were codependent and couldn't envision a life without the other person, that marriage is doomed.

I know when you're in love it's hard *not* to think of your guy as your very own Prince Charming who's going to make you eternally happy, but at some point reality is going to smack you in the face. For one thing, it's not your husband's job to make you happy. Moreover, *no one person can possibly fulfill all your deepest desires*. That's too much to put on one person. It sets up an impossible situation—for him and for you.

To be honest, there are going to be moments as a wife when you'll doubt your choice. Perhaps you'll see some sharp-jawed, blue-eyed male specimen picking out tomatoes in aisle 6 of your local grocery store and wonder if you made a mistake, or if you could have done better. Hollywood tells you these vulnerabilities indicate your relationship is on the rocks. It tells you no one in the *right* relationship ever doubts his or her decision. It tells you love comes in the shape of a six-pack and a sultry week in Cape Cod. But Hollywood only lasts two hours in the theater with a bag of overly buttered popcorn. Marriage lasts a lifetime.

Believe it or not, the folks who run Hollywood used to take their influence seriously. They used to produce films that were ethical and realistic, particularly when the theme was love. Take *Gone with the Wind*. In this film, the main character, Scarlett, is in love with Ashley. (Ashley is not a girl, by the way—you didn't think they had lesbian films in those days, did you?) Ashley loves Scarlett, too; but he's engaged to Melanie.

Scarlett knows Ashley's engaged to Melanie; but Scarlett has no scruples, so she throws herself at Ashley every chance she gets. And while he's hopelessly drawn to Scarlett, Ashley refuses her advances and insists he's better suited to Melanie—even though Melanie doesn't light his fire the way Scarlett does. What's important, Ashley says, is honor. Here's the exchange between them:

Ashley: I'm going to marry Melanie.

Scarlett: But you can't, not if you care for me!

Ashley: Oh my dear, why must you make me say things that will hurt you? How can I make you understand? You're so young and unthinking, you don't know what marriage means.

Scarlett: I know I love you and I want to be your wife! You don't love Melanie!

Ashley: She's like me, Scarlett. She's part of my blood. We understand each other.

Scarlett: But you love *me*!

Ashley: How could I help loving you? You have all the passion for life that I lack. But that kind of love isn't enough to make a successful marriage for two people who are as different as we are.[1]

In 1939, Hollywood was literally bound by contract to impart moral messages and avoid subjects that were considered improper. If *Gone with the Wind* had been made today, with the universal moral order no longer in place, Ashley and Scarlett would be involved in a torrid affair—before *and* after Ashley's marriage to Melanie.

I often wonder how many more successful marriages we'd have if people were exposed to films like *Gone with the Wind* instead of being fed a diet of modern-day "rom-coms." As I said in Step #1, the kind of support and camaraderie we experience in our lives significantly affects, for better or for worse, the decisions we make. It's not a coincidence the divorce rate was lower at a time when Hollywood produced films with strong moral messages.

Today, there's a whole new message coming out of Hollywood.

"Hollywood says you can be deeply in love with someone and then your marriage will work. But you can be deeply in love with someone to whom you cannot be successfully married," wrote Father Pat Connor.[2] Father Connor is a seventy-nine-year-old priest and counselor from Australia who speaks to high school seniors, mostly girls, about "whom not to marry." One of the things he tells them is that in most cases, infatuation trumps judgment.

If you're hesitant to take advice about marriage from a priest since he doesn't have firsthand experience, you may find it interesting that Connor's message mirrors Dr. M. Scott Peck's. Now deceased, Dr. Peck authored the bestselling book, first published in 1978, called *The Road Less Traveled*. It stayed on the *The New York Times* bestseller list for years. I was in college, in the mid-to-late '80s, when I first read it. What I remember most about it is the section on love. Specifically, the section on real love versus "falling in love."

"Of all the misconceptions about love," wrote Peck, "one of the most powerful and pervasive is the belief that 'falling in love' is love." There are two problems with this view, he said. The first is that the experience of falling in love is a "sex-linked erotic experience." The second is that it's "invariably temporary."[3]

No matter whom we fall in love with, Peck continued, "we sooner or later fall out of love if the relationship continues long enough . . . The feeling of ecstatic lovingness that characterizes love always passes. The honeymoon always ends. The bloom of romance always fades."[4] That was Ashley's point in *Gone with the Wind*: he knew the chemistry between Scarlett and him would fade, and they'd have nothing left to sustain them.

That our initial chemistry with a person ends sounds depressing, I know. That's not the way most of us probably wish it were. It must be even harder for someone in your generation to accept since you've been raised in a disposable world. Everything you desire is just a click away—and when you no longer want it, you just throw it out and find something else.

What this means for many people is that the moment their relationship hits a snag, the appeal of someone new—the desire for that "first kiss tingle" I heard Ryan Seacrest refer to once—can be overwhelming. But if you give in to it, you're buying yourself a boatload of trouble because you will never be satisfied. The same thing will happen over and over again with each new relationship.

Don't make the mistake so many people do. Don't assume that because the "feeling of ecstatic lovingness" ends, you've resigned yourself to boring sex or a dead love life. Relationships are designed to move on to the next phase. Your desire for your husband isn't going to end; it'll just take on a different feel. (If you genuinely feel nothing for him, that's one thing; but if the feelings were once there, they're probably still there.) No two people can sustain that initial level of excitement for decades—it's impossible. So just know that going in.

Once you accept that "falling in love" is not love, that it's merely step one of what has the potential to become real love, your perspective on marriage changes dramatically. As Peck wrote in the opening paragraphs of his book, "Once we know that life is difficult—once we truly understand and accept it—then life is no longer difficult. Because once it is accepted, the fact that life is difficult no longer matters."[5]

See what I mean? Whether we're talking about life being difficult or the fact that falling in love isn't love, the answer lies in the decision to accept *what is* rather than hold on to a false version of what you want it to be. If you do, then down the road, when you've been married awhile, you don't freak out. You don't assume your marriage is doomed because you've lost that "first kiss tingle."

That's one of the reasons so many Hollywood marriages—and marriages in which women are trying to emulate Hollywood marriages—fail. When the feelings of ecstasy reach their expiration date, as they always do, people assume the marriage is over. They built their lives on a fantasy.

I did that once—built my life on a fantasy. Only in my case it wasn't the "first kiss tingle" that consumed me; it was the idea that love conquered all. What Ashley said about passionate love not being enough to make a marriage work? He was right. I loved my first husband passionately. We weren't right for each other for a thousand different reasons, but I honestly believed I could love him so hard he'd eventually become the person I wanted him to be—as if I had the power to mold him like a piece of clay.

How ridiculous! How presumptuous! How stupid. But I know I'm not alone—countless women have made this same mistake. Too bad Father Connor hadn't shared his words of wisdom with my high school class. If he had, I might have seen the freight train coming before it left the station.

I met the man I would eventually marry in 1986, when I was a freshman at Boston University. Chris was a junior transfer student assigned to the same floor. He hailed from New York, while I had flown east from St. Louis, Missouri.

We met within the first month of school and became fast friends. At least that's all we thought it was until one night several months later when we found ourselves locked in a bathroom for well over an hour at the house of a mutual friend. We must have arrived at the bathroom at the same time—I can't remember—and the next thing we knew, we were kissing. That night our relationship turned romantic, and soon we became inseparable.

So inseparable, in fact, that within a year I had gone home with Chris to meet his family; and the following year he flew home to St. Louis with me. If that sounds fast, keep in mind we lived on the same floor and saw each other daily. We also had mutual friends, so we spent a fair amount of time in groups as well as alone.

Chris and I were together throughout my entire four years of college, even after he had graduated and moved back to New York to begin his financial career. We took shuttles back and forth between Boston and New York to see each other, or Chris would drive the eight hours there and back to see me.

After I graduated, Chris moved back to Boston to try to find a job because that's where we both decided we wanted to live. I'm sure we discussed marriage, but it wasn't a pressing matter; we just wanted to be together and were trying to figure out the logistics. Since we were raised in two different parts of the country, it wasn't easy. In fact, geography would prove to be the crux of our problems. It reared its ugly head on countless occasions, in various ways, over the years.

I got a teaching job in Cambridge after graduation, as well as an apartment and a roommate. Afterward, Chris came to Boston while he looked for a job. But after several months, he couldn't find one. So when a friend back in New York offered him a job, he felt he had no choice but to take it. Looking back, I think that decision marked the beginning of the end for us.

As it happens, my own job wasn't working out—for reasons unrelated to this story—so I quit. And I remember feeling a sense of inertia: I had no idea what to do next. That's when Chris suggested I move to New York and live with him. Well, that didn't sit well with me at all, which put me in even more of a pickle. I remember thinking: *Do I try to find another job in Boston now that Chris has moved back to New York? What would be the point? The allure of Boston involved him, and he isn't here. So now what? Do I move home to St. Louis, or do I move to New York and live with Chris?*

On that last point I was adamant: no. That may sound strange to someone of your generation, but people didn't live together in the early '90s the way they do today. Some did, but it wasn't the *norm*. It's true Chris and I had shared an apartment during the two summers before he graduated, but it was for a finite period of time—less than three months— and it involved roommates.

What Chris was suggesting was something different, and my thinking was: *Well, if he doesn't know he wants to marry me after four years together, he isn't going to be any more certain if I move in with him.* Somehow, even then, I knew cohabitation was counterproductive if the goal was ultimately to get married. With our relationship still in place (though clearly losing ground), I moved back home to St. Louis and in with my parents.

Which is why what happened next makes perfect sense. With Chris in New York and me in St. Louis, our relationship was going nowhere. We knew we couldn't make things work long-distance, so we had two choices: break up—or get engaged. We chose the latter.

Four years (and no kids) later, we were divorced.

To this day, I try not to think of my marriage to Chris as a mistake. I know people talk about their failed marriages as a "learning experience," one they wouldn't trade for anything because they learned so much about themselves, and if they hadn't made that choice, they wouldn't be where they are today, blah, blah, blah. But the truth is, I *do* regret marrying Chris. Nothing good happened after the wedding—well, other than the honeymoon. In fact, our honeymoon is the last truly happy time I remember.

I should have seen it coming, given how the engagement took place. It's not like Chris decided he wanted to marry me and went out searching for a ring. Rather, I was visiting him at his apartment in New York one weekend shortly after I had moved back home, and we were sitting on his couch for hours, talking about our relationship. By the end of that conversation, we were engaged.

Pretty romantic, huh? Of course, I see now what I couldn't see then. We got engaged because we didn't know what else to do. We wanted to be together and didn't know how to make sense of the conflicts we had. Were they an omen? Or were they things that could be resolved with enough effort and ingenuity? Chris was more practical about the matter, as men typically are, but I was a hopeless romantic and insisted we could work things out. That Chris loved me very deeply didn't hurt my case. I think I used his love for me, unknowingly, to talk him into marriage.

I'm not sure that's how *he'd* describe what happened, but somehow, some way, we came to the conclusion that if we just got married and were finally living in the same state, things would work out. And they did. For a while. But our marriage would be tested in a number of ways, much of it having to do with my living in a city I didn't want to live in and having few friends and family nearby. I felt like I was joining Chris on *his* venture, but there was no reciprocity.

That's what the fights were mostly about: my not fitting in to his world, and his unwillingness to compromise. Simply put, we came from two different worlds. Did you see the movie *Sweet Home Alabama*? It was like that, with Chris being like the Andrew character (except his family isn't wealthy or in politics), and my being like the Melanie character who was torn between two worlds: the big life up East vs. the simple life back home.

In both stories, home won.

I loved New York—at first. Chris and I spent loads of time there during the years we were together, and he taught me everything I know about the city. When he was working there and I was still in school, we'd meet in Grand Central Station at the Oyster Bar. Those were fantastic times. Life was full of promise.

But for me, the fantasy of New York would quickly diminish as the reality of its lifestyle set in. Chris and I fought constantly about traffic, tolls, and commuting. I never understood how people could waste so much time transporting themselves from point A to point B—we didn't do that in the Midwest. It wasn't just the time factor but the stress it caused. I had never seen anyone get so angry behind a wheel as Chris would.

But these things were normal to him. His father commuted to Manhattan his entire life and rarely made it home for dinner. That's just the way it was. That it didn't *have* to be that way, that we could build a different life somewhere else if we wanted, didn't interest Chris. In every conceivable way, his heart was in New York. No other city offered what he was looking for. Chris was going all the way to the top, and New York was the only place to do that.

Indeed, Chris was a highly ambitious man. I didn't think anything of this at first because I like an ambitious person. *I'm* ambitious. But his ambition was on another level altogether. Everything Chris did, he did to the max: studying, working, even partying. It was like he was in his own zone and would welcome anyone who wanted to join him; but if the other person had a mission of his or her own, forget it. Nothing and no one was going to get in his way. In retrospect, he just wasn't ready to be married. That's all there is to it.

Which is just as well, since even if he *had* been ready, we wouldn't have done well together. My antenna had gone up on countless occasions during the course of our relationship—especially when the subject of children, religion, or politics came up. Unfortunately, it took starting a life together for the two of us to accept that he and I had entirely different values. The things that were important to him weren't important to me, and vice versa. The things I believed in he didn't believe in, and vice versa. The way he handled problems and unforeseen conflicts was not the way I handled them. But in my romantic head, up until the last possible moment, I thought I could change him.

Please read this carefully: you can never, *ever*, change your man. Ever. Did I say *ever*? Ever. You can't love a man so hard and so well that your problems will magically disappear. You can't convince him to see life your way if he doesn't. And you won't be the one person who will prove it can be done—your relationship is no more special than mine was. There was no lack of love between Chris and me. That's the one thing, maybe the only thing, we did have. Bottom line: if you don't love a man *exactly as he is*, even if he never changes a stinkin' thing, get out.

Father Connor addressed this point in his speech to young women. Here's some of what he said, paraphrased:

- Don't marry a problem character thinking you'll change him—for example, if he's a heavy drinker, don't think that if he just marries a good woman, he'll settle down. People are the same after marriage as before, only more so.

- Never marry a man who has no friends.

- Examine his nature. Does he possess those character traits that add up to a good human being? Conversely, do you see "red flag" behaviors? For example, is he inclined to fits of rage? If so, is he capable of admitting his faults and apologizing? If warning flags are waving in the wind, stay away!

- Take a good, unsentimental look at his family. Are his parents married or divorced? If your guy is a product of divorce, that may—indeed, probably will—bring with it a whole host of issues. If his parents *are* married, what is their marriage like? Does your guy have a good relationship with his parents?

There are so many things that aren't obvious when you're in love. In its early stages, love really is blind. But none of the points above should be ignored, particularly the part about your boyfriend's family of origin. I suspect most people have "issues" of one sort or another with their parents, but what really matters are the messages about life and love that get passed on from parents to children. Ask yourself whether you agree with and respect the ones your boyfriend's parents passed on to him.

The third point Father Connor made, to "examine his nature," is also important. You need to be aware of how your boyfriend or fiancé reacts to things. Is he easily bothered or quick to anger? Is he compassionate and loving toward other people—not just you? Does he tend to be self-absorbed? Watch how he handles people: his co-workers, his boss, his nieces and nephews, even strangers. That should tell you a lot.

Over the course of my relationship with Chris there were many red flags. But I lacked the courage to face them. We were the opposite of those characters in the old movies, the ones who faced their conflicts squarely in the eye and moved on. Sometimes when you get so deep in a relationship, it's hard to believe life exists outside that person or that there could be someone else out there who's better suited for you. Or sometimes, let's face it: you just don't *want* to let him (or her) go. You love him and you want to be with him, and that's all there is to it.

So instead of facing the music, we focused on the good stuff—of which there was plenty. Chris was, at heart, a very good man: he was loyal; he never cheated or lied; and he was affectionate and open with his feelings. He was very good to me for a long time, and he loved me very much. He loved me *despite* my flaws, which as far as I'm concerned is enough to reel anyone in. I was smitten. But in the end, it came down to two different people from two different worlds who wanted two very different lives.

Step #4 is simple to understand but hard to accept: When choosing a husband, *you cannot rely on love.* If you fall in love with a man whose values and priorities differ sharply from yours, you will waste valuable time and energy, and invite a boatload of heartache to boot, trying to make the relationship into something it's not. Marriage is work, yes. But you shouldn't have to work at having the same values. You either share them, or you don't.

You have to forget about romantic love when it comes to choosing a spouse. Romance may be the path to a fun or even satisfying dating relationship, and it can certainly be the *start* of something potentially lasting, but it has nothing to do with sustaining a marriage. My advice to you is to keep your feelings in perspective. You may love someone deeply.

But that's no reason to marry him.

*Step #5*

# GET A RING,
# NOT A ROOMMATE

I KNOW I TOLD YOU my ex-husband wanted us to live together before we married, and I refused to do so. And I know he and I went ahead and got married only to wind up divorced, but don't assume that means we would have been better off living together. *There is no way to know whether a guy is right for you or not by living with him first.*

Cohabitation may be commonplace—it has increased in the United States over the past half century by more than 1,500 percent[1]—and thus seems benign. But that doesn't mean it *is* benign. Just because something's popular doesn't mean it's right—that was the point of Step #1. To make good decisions, you must be able to step away from the prevailing culture and think for yourself. You must ask yourself, "Is this smart? Does this feel right *in my gut*? Will this get me where I ultimately want to go?"

There are two main reasons people live together. Convenience is the most obvious. Since couples are sleeping over at each other's apartments every night anyway, they figure they can save a lot of time and money if they rent one apartment. The second reason couples move in together is to determine whether or not they're compatible.

If only it were that simple. The truth is, living with someone does not offer a couple the assurances they're looking for. Cohabitation is, in fact, *counterproductive* to a successful marriage. The best research to date on this subject can be found in the ongoing study called the National Marriage Project. A nonpartisan, nonsectarian, and interdisciplinary initiative, the NMP was founded in 1997 by Drs. Popenoe and Barbara Dafoe Whitehead. Its mission is to provide research and analysis on the health of marriage in America, to analyze the social and cultural forces shaping contemporary marriage, and to identify strategies to increase marital quality and stability.

One of its findings is that living together before marriage—*unless the couple was engaged beforehand*—increases the risk of divorce. "The longer you live together with a partner," wrote Popenoe, "the more likely it is that the low-commitment ethic of cohabitation will take hold."[2] In other words, people who are used to living together never acquire the tools they need to stay the course because they always have an out. Their commitment to the relationship is therefore more fragile.

And commitment is really the issue. Cohabitation is simply commitment with an escape hatch—which, by that very definition, means it's not a commitment. It's also something people tend to fall into. A marriage, on the other hand, is a *decision* people make. Those are two very different things.

So why do people choose to cohabitate? What's the goal? Research shows women are more likely to view cohabitation as a step toward marriage, while men are likelier to see it as a way to postpone commitment. "This gender asymmetry is associated with negative interactions and lower levels of commitment even after the relationship progresses to marriage," wrote Meg Jay in *The New York Times*.[3]

Here's something else to think about. When cohabiting couples break up and marry other people, they bring a great deal of baggage to their new marriages—which initially feel a lot like their previous cohabiting relationship. As someone who brought some very heavy baggage from an actual marriage to another one, trust me: you don't want to do this. Just because things are going well for me now doesn't mean my marriage has been a cakewalk. It has not.

Let me tell you the two main reasons you should not live with a man to whom you are not engaged. First, *it does not allow for the objectivity you'll need in trying to determine whether or not he's "the one."* The reason the statistics make an exception for couples who were engaged before they moved in together is because the weight of the decision about whom to marry rests on the day the choice is made. Most cohabitating couples haven't made any decision at all. They're just playing house.

But if you've already made the decision about whom to marry, moving in together before the wedding is not all that significant to the health of the marriage. If you *haven't* made up your mind, if you're still deciding whether or not he's the one, living with him isn't going to help you make up your mind. On the contrary, it will cloud your judgment. You'll just get in deeper and deeper until eventually you can't see the forest through the trees. Living in separate spaces makes it much easier to make an informed decision.

And objectivity is crucial when it comes to choosing a spouse. There are plenty of ways people lack objectivity even without cohabitating, such as the woman who's desperate for a baby or who's already pregnant. Getting married under these circumstances usually doesn't bode well for making a good choice of partner.

Or take my own situation. I lacked objectivity the first time I got married not because I was pregnant, or desperate for a baby, or even living with Chris, but because I was living with my parents and felt trapped. Those circumstances were directly related to my belief that love was enough to make a marriage work. Simply put, I wanted out—and as a result talked myself into the idea of marrying Chris. If I had not been living with my parents, if Chris and I had lived in the same city in separate apartments, I suspect we both would have come to a different conclusion about our relationship.

Or take this woman I heard about, Anna, who said she lived with her ex-husband before they got married and felt she was auditioning to be his wife. "We shared everything: furniture, bank accounts, animals, etc. By the time we hit our thirties, the next logical step was to get married." The decision to get married in situations like Anna's is haphazard: it just happens. It is not purposeful, the way getting engaged is supposed to be.

Getting married as a default mechanism—because it seems like the next step, because someone wants a baby, because you're already living together and, what the hell? Why not?—will almost always result in an unhappy ending. In such circumstances, marriage becomes a crapshoot rather than a commitment. A commitment is a decision made. The other is happenstance.

The second reason you should not live with someone to whom you're not engaged is because *there's a psychological process that takes place once a decision is made.* The way two people approach a marriage in which they assume they'll be together until "death do us part" is very different from a relationship in which the end is unknown. "The very option of being allowed to change our minds," wrote Barry Schwartz, "seems to increase the chances we *will* change our minds. When we can change our minds about decisions, we are less satisfied with them. When a decision is final, we engage in a variety of psychological processes that enhance our feelings about the choice we made relative to the alternatives."[4]

This is one of the reasons, perhaps the main reason, so many cohabitating partners don't make it to the altar.

The choice about whom to marry has rarely been so tenuous. It used to be common, for example, for young people to seek their parents' advice and approval before becoming engaged. This may seem archaic to us, but it was sound practice. Parents can generally see what their grown children cannot since they're not emotionally invested in the relationship. Unfortunately, this practice went the way of the dinosaur. Being products of the divorce generation, young people can rarely rely on their parents' good advice. Their *grand*parents', perhaps. But not their parents'.

There's also this: while modern women pretend to be fine with shacking up, I don't buy it. Lack of commitment makes women uneasy. Remember: a woman's desire to bond is more pronounced than a man's. So no matter how content a woman may appear to be in a cohabitating relationship, deep down what she really wants is a ring. She wants a commitment. She wants to know she has someone there every night. Permanently.

A man's incentive to marry is different. Remember: men are hunters. They want love, too; but the longer they can postpone commitment, the longer many of them will. Ultimately, a man's desire to marry stems from his "need to choose a particular woman and stay by her and provide for her if he is to know his children and they are to love him and call him father," wrote Discovery Institute founder George Gilder in *Men and Marriage.* "Marriage asks men to give up their essential sexuality only as part of a clear scheme for replacing it with new, far more important roles: husband and father."[5]

That's not to say there aren't cohabitating couples where the man wants to get married and the woman doesn't, but it's less common. Regardless of who's holding back, though, the reason is generally the same: fear of divorce, or fear that they're settling for less than they deserve. Or both. Remember: the modern generation has been taught they're entitled to perfection. So when they get a partner with flaws, which is the only kind to get, they question the entire relationship. They allow their fear of dissatisfaction to take over.

Your story can be different. All you have to do is reject the idea that cohabitation is harmless. If marriage is the goal, living with someone is not going to help you get there. It's like I said about sex. If you hold high standards for yourself, standards that *aren't* commensurate with pop culture, you're less likely to become part of the statistics.

Remember that men aren't programmed to commit—and playing house won't change their minds. If lasting love is the goal, you need a ring, not a roommate.

*Step #6*

# REJECT THE GREEN
# GRASS SYNDROME

I'LL JUST COME OUT and say it. *You will never get everything you want all wrapped up in one man.* It doesn't matter whom you end up with—John Doe or Brad Pitt—there will always be something missing. Always. If this is a phenomenon you can't get your head around, you are not alone. You're suffering from an affliction your generation knows well. It's called the *Green Grass Syndrome.*

The Green Grass Syndrome can apply to any choice we make in life—whether it's which item to order on the menu, which pair of jeans to buy, or which man to marry. I know it's unpleasant to think about marriage in this way, but the process is very similar. When it comes to choosing a husband, you must (a) decide what you need and (b) ignore the rest. Because the man you pick, no matter who he is, will have deficiencies.

But guess what? So do you.

That will be especially hard for your generation to accept since you've been raised to think you're perfect just the way you are. Nobody has to *do* anything to be important anymore—you're important just for being born. "Never settle for less than the best!" you were told. "You *deserve* it." Consequently, young people set their sights insanely high—which means every potential mate seems substandard.

The Green Grass Syndrome is particular relevant to girls. As we covered in Step #2, the manner in which girls are raised today is unprecedented—and it's a result of the fusion of two movements: the feminist movement and the self-esteem movement. These two worldviews are so hopelessly similar they're impossible to extricate. Feminism says, "Your mothers' lives were constrained. Don't live their lives—reach for the stars instead!" And the self-esteem movement says, "There's no one quite like you. You're *amazing*. Go—seize the world."

The implication is that women are entitled to lives that defy description. They should be out-of-this-world exciting. It's a message that gets delivered to women's doorsteps every day via their televisions. Programs that portray a female character living a whirlwind life of sex, fantasy, and riches are a dime a dozen. Together, they provide a breeding ground for the Green Grass Syndrome.

Initially, the self-esteem movement seemed harmless. One might think, "How can it be bad to encourage young women to shoot for the stars?" But it can. For one thing, assuming that every girl (or boy, for that matter) should be, or even *can* be, president, or a movie star, or even a CEO, is elitist. The implication is that the lives of these folks are somehow superior. As if people who live regular lives, or—God forbid—have blue-collar jobs that don't require a college degree, are somehow "less than." When this perspective is taught, children grow up believing recognition and appearance are more important than working hard, refining a skill set, or just living by the golden rule.

Moreover, the kind of lives toward which we're steering women don't even represent the lives most people live. The only reason it seems as though everyone's living an exciting life is because television makes it look that way. But the folks on TV represent the *minority*. For every one famous person, there are maybe a hundred thousand regular people. Most people in the limelight don't even live lives you would want. Nothing is ever what it seems. Remember: it's all a mirage.

Why do we insist on steering young women in the wrong direction? We should be teaching them how to find meaning in everyday life. It should be more than enough to find a loving spouse, raise a couple of great kids, find meaningful work, and have good friends. The research shows this is what makes people happiest anyway.

As it is, modern women think if they don't do something monumental, their lives are meaningless. They think if they don't marry a Rob Lowe, they're "settling." As twenty-something Rachel Weight wrote in an article entitled "How *The Notebook* Has Ruined Me": "I think movies like this may have ruined me. Under their influence, I now expect a formula for my romantic life."[1]

Indeed. And that formula—hot Hollywood man/hot Hollywood sex—will lead to some serious disappointment down the road. How many of us can possibly have sex in the manner Noah and Allie did for years on end? You may say you know that's impossible, that *The Notebook* is just a movie; but a steady diet of this stuff is going to influence people. There's no way around it.

What women don't realize is that even if they do get everything they *think* they want, the joy is short-lived. Once the high wears off—and it will, as we learned in Step #4—women will want something they've been told all their lives they should have: more. But for those who suffer from the Green Grass Syndrome, the grass is always, always, *always* greener on the other side of the fence—even if you're married to Ryan Gosling. Hard to believe, but it's true.

Did you see the movie *Mona Lisa Smile*? The one set in the 1950s that starred Julia Roberts? This film's message is that rather than "just" get married and have babies—how boring—women should travel the world, run companies, be sexually liberated, become president! Whatever she does, a woman should not become a wife and mother, or housewife as they called it then. By liberating herself from this prism, any woman can live a life equivalent to a movie star's!

This new way of thinking was designed to get women to think outside the marriage-and-motherhood box . . . which wasn't a bad thing in and of itself. But it went too far. This feminist message was later exacerbated by self-esteem rhetoric, as well as an economic boom, in which the drive for "bigger, better, more" became palpable. The result is a self-absorbed, narcissistic generation that thinks they're entitled to anything they want.

Three excellent books expose this phenomenon. Two are by the same author— psychologist Jean Twenge—and are titled *Generation Me* and *The Narcissism Epidemic*. The other is *NurtureShock*, by Po Bronson and Ashley Merryman. Each book points out the harm excessive praise does to young people. "Sure, [your child] is special," wrote Bronson and Merryman, "but new research suggests that if you tell him that, you'll ruin him. It's a neurobiological fact."[2]

And women *have* been ruined, for they can't seem to "lower" themselves to an everyday existence. How can the modern woman pick a regular ole guy and live a regular ole life when her entire life she's been told there's a world out there so exciting that it exceeds her wildest dreams? The culture insists it's all about choice and the liberation it brings. But too much choice can cause people to develop inertia and ultimately leads to the Green Grass Syndrome. No one decision is ever good enough.

To make matters worse, our lax divorce culture makes it easy for husbands and wives to change their minds—and women are particularly susceptible to pulling the trigger. According to the National Marriage Project, two-thirds of all divorces are initiated by women.[3] Feminists will tell you this is because there are so many bad husbands in the world and that women have no choice. They want you to think men like Tiger Woods represent the average guy. But two-thirds of our nation's husbands are not sex addicts.

So how can you avoid the Green Grass Syndrome? The first thing you need to do is make a mental list of your wants and needs, and then write them down. As you peruse the list, try to think less about what you want and more about what you don't want, or what you absolutely can't live without. In other words, *decide what you need or must have.* Because you're never going to get everything on your list, you're going to have to take the good with the bad. You can't just have the fun and easy. You've got to settle into everyday life or you're going to be chronically dissatisfied.

When I met my second husband, I was twenty-nine. It was late at night—maybe even morning—and he'd arrived at the bar where I had serendipitously planted myself, despite my reservations about going out earlier that evening. He had just been to a wedding and was wearing a suit with one of those ocean-blue shirts that, at the time, were all the rage. He looked *good.*

But that only mildly interested me. Obviously, we all want (and need) to be attracted to someone in order to be interested in him or her—I had been on enough dates since my divorce to know what a lack of attraction felt like. Yuck. Nevertheless, what was on my radar at that point in my life (and on his, apparently) was family. Permanence. Commitment.

In other words, our attraction to each other was a given. But other things took precedence.

In thinking about my future, I knew what I wanted—and more importantly, what I *didn't* want. I knew that if I didn't find a man whose principles and priorities were similar to my own, our marriage wouldn't make it beyond the first anniversary. I also wanted a spouse who was flexible and easygoing. A chameleon type: someone who could go camping *or* attend a black tie event—and fit in either way. Someone who wanted to put family first, who had a strong faith in God, and who was capable of self-reflection.

I'm happy to report I have all that.

But, there are plenty of things I don't have. For example (and this is a small thing), I wish my husband did not do everything last minute. I can't tell you how many times he's been *in the shower* when company arrives—I used to get so mad. Now when people come over and ask where he is, I just smile and say he's in the shower, like it's the most natural thing in the world. Like everyone does that. I've come to accept this part of his personality because there's not a thing I can do about it.

My husband is also emotionally reserved. He can be very deadpan in his reactions, which leaves me wondering what he really thinks about something. I find his laid-back demeanor annoying. But wait. Didn't I say a moment ago that I wanted an easygoing guy? Why yes, I did. So I can hardly complain that my husband's easygoing when that's exactly what I said I wanted.

See how crazy it is? The desire to have everything seeks no end. But it's unrealistic to expect your guy (or gal) to have all the qualities on your list. That's why I'm suggesting you focus on your nonnegotiables, or the things you can't live without. Once you have those down, the rest you have to accept. Besides, there are plenty of things your husband's going to wish *you* were that you're not. The trick is not to hold these things against each other.

By the way, not to get all technical here, but there are actually terms for what we're talking about. "Maximizers" are people who obsess over every choice before and after making one, while "satisficers" are content with whatever decision they make. Barry Schwartz has argued in *The Paradox of Choice* that satisficers tend to be happier than maximizers because maximizers spend a great deal of time and energy reaching a decision and are often anxious about whatever decision they end up making. They're never satisfied.[4]

If you want to be happily married, you're going to have to become a satisficer.

The second thing you need to do to avoid the Green Grass Syndrome is *accept that what matters to you now likely won't mean beans down the road.* When you're young and not thinking about bills, kids, schools, or churches, it's easy to overlook the things that will matter later on. This is where maturity comes into play. It takes a big, fat dose of maturity to be able to think beyond tomorrow. What do you envision twenty years from now? Whatever it is, it needs to be considered alongside your feelings toward a potential husband.

Now I wish I could say the Green Grass Syndrome ends once you decide whom to marry. Unfortunately, it will most likely kick you again in the you-know-what down the road. You'll find your guy, and life will be great—for a while. Maybe even a long while. But at some point along the way, you and your husband will face some very real problems, and it is then that you may find yourself questioning your choice of a husband. Not in a bad, debilitating way (I hope), but in a general way. And when that happens, you may start to notice other people's husbands. After all, it's human nature to compare; and these comparisons happen most when problems arise. You may think to yourself, *Gee, why can't my husband be like that?*

And that's when you need to stop.

Don't go any further. When this happens, if it happens, you need to remember what I said at the beginning of this chapter. *No matter whom you marry, if you are a victim of the Green Grass Syndrome, the grass always looks greener on the other side of the fence.* You must also remember that these things you're noticing, whatever they may be, only seem greener. In truth, the grass on that other side is just as brown as it is on yours. Assuming this ahead of time allows you to get your mind off the other potential life and put it back on your life, where it belongs.

I truly believe this is where so many women get into trouble. Our divorce culture encourages women to search for something better when they're dissatisfied. I'm not saying the average woman treats her marriage with little regard. I'm saying that when the going gets tough, *and it will*, the culture in which we live helps push women out the door.

You need to understand what our culture won't tell you: when doubt creeps in, that doesn't mean your marriage is doomed or that you chose the wrong husband. Everyone has doubts. Absorb that fact. *Doubt is normal.* Human. But it won't be debilitating unless you let it.

In order to avoid this fate, you need a firm understanding of the Green Grass Syndrome—and then you need to reject it. Once you know these other husbands, or marriages, or lives are no better or worse than yours, your perspective will improve dramatically. Because the moment you say to yourself, "Hmm . . . I wonder if I'd be better off with that man," or, "I wonder if I'd be happier with that life," you'll remember that that man or life just looks better because it's new. In reality, both have just as many warts as yours. They're just different warts.

I can't tell you how important it is to understand this once you've made your decision about whom to marry. Honestly, I'd put money on the fact that at some point you're going to ask yourself if you married the right guy. Life is hard, and it's natural to want to bolt when things get tough. Only by avoiding the Green Grass Syndrome will you come out ahead.

Finally, keep in mind what I said about my own marriage: it is not a fairy tale. It has taken an enormous amount of emotional work on my part, as well as my husband's, to keep our marriage strong—if that's even the right word. Each of us came to our marriage with baggage. Not only was I divorced, my husband is a child of divorce—and this has brought with it a host of problems you wouldn't believe. Or maybe you would, if you're a child of divorce, too.

What I'm trying to say is that while my husband and I were fortunate to find each other, we don't rest on our laurels. Too many people think finding a spouse is about being in the right place at the right time, as if a husband or wife is just "out there" somewhere, waiting to be found—and that once you've found him or her, that's it. But the world is too big for such a notion. There are plenty of people with whom we might be well suited. It doesn't even make sense that there's only one person "out there" for every other one person.

It's our view of marriage as a vocation that keeps my husband and me chugging along. Our problems are no better or worse than anyone else's; we just work at them. It's not that we don't have issues that could potentially lead to divorce—we do. We're just cognizant of the Green Grass Syndrome. We don't believe there's a better life or better person out there for us. Things would have to be really, really bad before we'd get divorced. Really bad—not just, "I'm not happy with you anymore" or, "You just don't do it for me anymore" bad.

Step #6 can be summed up in one of several ways. *Decide what you need and ignore the rest. Reject the Green Grass Syndrome, or match your expectations with reality.* Take your pick. The point is, when you run into trouble in your marriage—and you will—look inward, not outward. Assume the answer to your problems lies within the marriage, not outside of it. Only then can you solve the real issues.

Research shows that most people who get divorced bring the same unresolved issues to their new marriages. That's because the problem wasn't necessarily the marriage, but the way the couple dealt with the problems within that marriage. More often than not, a new marriage will present just as many problems as the old.

Bottom line: We must stop instilling in women this idea that their lives have in store for them something profound, something magical, something so great it belies description. Unrealistic expectations set up a false reality, and real life can only be disappointing.

It's perfectly normal to wonder if the grass is greener in someone else's backyard, but it isn't normal to believe you've settled for a second-rate life. It isn't normal when this phenomenon absorbs you. That kind of thinking comes from cultural conditioning. Only by accepting that you're going to be dissatisfied *to some degree* no matter whom you marry—and that when this happens, someone else's life may seem more appealing—will the Green Grass Syndrome stop crippling women's lives.

It's a vicious cycle. That's why the goal should *not* be to have what you want—but to want what you have. You've probably heard that before. And now I'll close with this nugget of wisdom from Schwartz's book:

> A friend once told me how his minister had shocked the congregation with a sermon on marriage in which he said, flatly that, yes, the grass is always greener. What he meant was that you will encounter people who are younger, better looking, funnier, smarter, or seemingly more

understanding or empathetic than your wife or husband.

But finding a life partner is not a matter of comparison shopping or "trading up." The only way to find happiness and stability in the presence of seemingly attractive and tempting options is to say, "I'm simply not going there. I've made my decision about a life partner, so this person's empathy or that person's looks really have nothing to do with me. I'm not in the market—end of story."[5]

# *Step #7*

# MARRY THE ACCOUNTANT, NOT THE ARTIST

THIS CHAPTER, I'M AFRAID, is the part where we talk about money. Ugh. It's such a dreaded subject, isn't it? Who wants to think about money when we're talking about love? But that's just it: people *aren't* thinking about it. Not in the way they should.

When I consider the significance of money in a marriage, I'm reminded of something Lori Gottlieb wrote in *Marry Him*. She said she essentially woke up one day to find herself unhappily single at the age of forty. In her analysis of why it happened, she wrote that when she was in her twenties, her mother told her to stop going out with those artist boyfriends she liked so much. She said Lori should find herself a man with a steady job, maybe one of those guys she thought was nerdy but who turned out well on all fronts. Naturally, Gottlieb thought this was a bunch of old-fashioned drivel.

Then she wrote how stupid she was to reject her mother's advice.

That's how I came to title Step #7, "Marry the Accountant, Not the Artist." You can substitute "accountant" with any job or career that brings in a steady income. The point isn't to focus on the *kind* of job a man has (after all, some artists make good money!); it's to point out that your guy needs to be employed, or to at least have a legitimate plan for legitimate employment.

I'll say it again: the previous generation of American women was wrong. You *will* need, and want, to depend on a man at some point in your life. You need someone who can bring home the bacon so you can fry it up in a pan. Even if you don't cook. He doesn't need to make a ton of money, but he needs to make enough—or be capable of making enough—to keep the family afloat.

As usual, this goes against everything your generation has been taught. In fact, if your friends heard me say this, they'd be shocked and even offended. "How retro! Who thinks that way anymore? What a loon." Well, they're certainly entitled to their opinion.

Even if it *is* wrong.

The reason parents have historically taught their daughters to look for a man who can support them (until the sexual revolution came along to muck things up) is because they assumed their girls would be home with their children when the time came and would therefore need husbands who made enough money to support the family. And while it's true things have changed with respect to women's employment status, maternal desire hasn't changed one bit. "So many of us were schooled to be professionals of some sort," wrote Kathryn Lopez. "We were prepped and we excelled. But that degreed and résuméd woman doesn't cease being who she was before she had a baby."[1]

It doesn't matter whether it's 1955 or 2013—human nature is human nature. In the past, women *and men* prepared for the day when babies would arrive. Today we do not. Since women are taught to pursue careers with the same verve as men, couples assume they'll both be in the workforce their entire lives—every day, all year long. As a result, women set aside *zero* space for motherhood, and that is why they no longer search for husbands who can support them. "We can take care of ourselves!" they insist.

This is the dumbest approach to life I've ever heard.

Liberated or not, the vast majority of women choose to quit their jobs or cut back when they have children. For some, it happens right away. For others, it takes the birth of a second or third child. Regardless, most women do not stay in the workforce the way men do: full-time, year-round, year after year after year.

Naturally, this puts the modern woman in a precarious position since she made plans for a completely different life. Many women, when they were dating, ignored their boyfriends' financial potential. Their beaus also assumed their girlfriends would become working mothers. That's the modern-day plan.

Take Laurie Tennant, whose life as a working mother seemed to be working out fine: "I felt perfectly balanced," she said. It wasn't until her second child came, when Tennant was home on another maternity leave, that she had the opportunity to spend a considerable amount of time with her first child, who was by then several years older. Tennant was "jolted by how much she enjoyed the experience."[2] Shortly thereafter, she quit her job.

The single greatest mistake modern women make is mapping out their lives according to their big career plans and paying no attention to how these plans will coordinate with the other aspects of their lives—namely, marriage and motherhood. They should do the exact opposite: put marriage and motherhood (along with homemaking, friendships, exercise, etc.), not career, at the center of their lives and fit everything else in around that. Because the reality is, if you plan to be physically and emotionally present in your children's lives, you're going to need a husband you can depend on financially. Most men want to take care of their wife and kids, remember? This arrangement is neither foolish nor backward.

It's smart.

Americans have been sold a myth when it comes to work and family. We're told the difference between women who stay home when they have children and women who don't is that some women just *like* being around kids all the time, as if some are cut out for this role and others aren't. People assume the more education a woman has, the less likely she is to assume such a menial role—as though mothering one's own children is beneath an educated woman.

What bunk. When women become mothers, they change—emotionally and physiologically. What separates the women who choose to stay home from those who do not is twofold. Either they planned to do so from the get-go and made decisions accordingly, or they ignore social trends and go with their gut. They listen to what their hearts tell them to do. Being "cut out for it" is neither here nor there.

That's not to say some women don't love staying home and choose to make a career out of it. My friend Lila, for example, is a mother of seven. Having a big family has always been her dream. But she's unusual. Most mothers who stay home do so not because they want to be mothers exclusively but because they want motherhood to be a major part of their lives—and because they believe staying home is the right thing to do.

Other women make the decision to stay home when they realize daycare isn't cost-effective. A woman has to make some serious bucks to offset the costs incurred by living a dual-income lifestyle, at least when she has babies and toddlers at home. Unless the wife makes a six-figure salary, the money from a second income is usually eaten up by commuting costs, child care, eating out, work attire, dry cleaning, convenience foods, and, of course, taxes. By the time you add it up, there isn't much left.

It's not just the money, either. Women have incurred an even greater loss by the new lifestyle they've created: the loss of time. My friend Jane lost her job recently as a sales rep for a pharmaceutical company. She has two beautiful girls, ages five and nine, and she's never been unemployed as an adult. One of the main things she noticed about her new life is that she isn't always rushing off somewhere. All of a sudden the world opened up to her. She has *time*.

Maybe Jane will start a home business one day. Perhaps she'll become a gourmet cook. She may get more involved in her children's school. Maybe she'll get a part-time job or learn a language. Or maybe she'll simply hang out with her children and soak up the short time she has left with them before they grow up. The point is, whatever she chooses, the reason she *has* the choice is because she and her husband were smart: they didn't make financial decisions based on being a two-income family. That's what you should do, too.

The desire to have a life outside of work has been the subject of media attention as of late. A recent article in *The Wall Street Journal* highlighted women, even single women, who are officially fed up with their all-consuming lifestyle of work, work, work. These ladies make big bucks, but they want their lives back. They want time to bike, have coffee with friends, cook, exercise, and travel for pleasure instead of work.

Which goes back to my point about depending on a man. If you want a balanced life, you're going to *have* to depend on a man. Men's goals are, for the most part, simpler and more straightforward. "Men are driven by who they are, what they do, and how much they make. No matter if a man is a CEO, a CON, or both, everything he does is filtered through his title (who he is), how he gets that title (what he does), and the reward he gets for the effort (how much he makes.) These three things make up the basic DNA of manhood," wrote Steve Harvey.[3]

Now, please don't start tallying up all the guys you know who don't fall into this category—there are always exceptions. But generally speaking, men don't feel good about themselves if their salaries aren't substantial enough to support a family.

Unfortunately, men don't get the opportunity to *be* the breadwinner these days because women are competing for this role. As I've mentioned, most couples assume women will remain in the workforce their entire lives and plan accordingly. This impractical approach to family life can cause enormous conflict once couples become parents and see for themselves what's involved in caring for children and maintaining a home. The two-income lifestyle may be a win-win when children aren't in the picture—there's even a name for that: DINK (dual income, no kids)—but throw kids into the equation, and it's a whole different ballgame.

Can you imagine how much easier it would be for women to assume ahead of time that for X number of years they will need, and want, to depend on a husband? If their assumptions about their lives are reversed—if women assume they *will* be home at some point, not that they won't—they can map out their lives in a way that allows this to happen. A man's linear career goals and a woman's maternal desire should be front and center in young people's minds no matter how "liberated" they think they are.

That doesn't mean women need to marry rich men. In fact, if you *do* go that route, you may end up feeling like a single mom. If you marry a CEO, big-time lawyer, brain surgeon, etc., your husband will rarely be home—and you need to be okay with that. You can't choose to marry a man whose work life is all consuming and then complain later on that he's never home.

That was one of my biggest concerns about Chris. His priorities were clear from the get-go: he was going all the way to the top. Once it became evident just *how* committed he was to that goal, I realized I didn't trust that his priorities would change. I thought he'd get in deeper and deeper, which he did.

Other women may not mind that in a husband. Maybe they like the idea of a rich husband, even if it means he's rarely home or not that involved on the home front. Perhaps they've always longed for a high-falutin lifestyle and are willing to accept the trade-offs. There's nothing wrong with that—it just wasn't for me.

Factoring in a man's earning potential has an added benefit: it allows men to take care of women. And that, as I said earlier, is what most men want to do. Men are made to protect, provide, and defend. That's what they do, and most of them do it well when given the opportunity. Unfortunately, feminists have convinced Americans that if society would liberate women from the "burden" of caring for home, husband, and children and in turn would liberate men from the "burden" of producing an income, equality would prevail and life would be grand.

But feminists are fighting Mother Nature, and they can't win. If you stay out of it, a whole new world will open up to you. If you let a man take care of you, you may find you like it. There's even a word for it: *hypergamy*. Hypergamy is marriage to someone of equal or higher status. For women, this desire is instinctive; and it's a centuries-old phenomenon. You're probably aware of the articles in the last few years that ask the question, "Where have the good men gone?" What this question really means is: "Where are all the men of my equal status or higher?"

And the answer is simple: women drove them away. The reason there are fewer successful men today is because women have been competing with men on the same level. They've knocked men off their pedestals (even though women have their own pedestals to perch upon) and climbed up to take what feminists insisted was rightfully theirs. Ergo, men are floundering.

Have you read the Fifty Shades trilogy? The first novel in the series, *Fifty Shades of Grey*, is a fantastic illustration of hypergamy. If you haven't read it, I wouldn't recommend it for a number of reasons. But it's really the relationship between the book's two main characters, Christian Grey and Anastasia Steele, that interested me. Anastasia is a soon-to-be college graduate who interviews the fabulously wealthy entrepreneur Christian Grey. The story itself is completely unrealistic, mind you—not only is Grey beautiful, he owns (and flies) his own helicopter. At *twenty-six*. But the book's allure is real. Women ate it up.

Anastasia, or "Ana," as she is called, is an old-fashioned "good" girl. At twenty-two, she's a virgin and has never been drunk. Ana is also smart, fiercely independent, and a great match for Christian. Christian wants Ana desperately, but on his own terms. He represents the opposite of the modern American man: he's highly successful, as opposed to being a slacker; and rather than being emasculated, he's clear about what he wants. And what he wants is for Ana to be submissive. He also wants her to dress in a more feminine manner.

Despite her reservations, Ana finds herself drawn to Christian and is intrigued by the idea of submission. But here's the thing: Christian doesn't *demand* that Ana be submissive—he *asks* her to be. Ana has complete free will: she can decide to oblige or she can tell him to go jump in a lake. And while the concept of submission goes against every fiber of her being, Ana surrenders. The theme of *Fifty Shades of Grey* is trust. It's about women being nurturing and men taking charge, and how the natural love of a good woman can make a strong man fall in love with her.

*Fifty Shades of Grey* is a great example of the innate differences between women and men, and how they can work in tandem. Don't get carried away with the analogy, though—Christian's not your typical male. He's so driven by lust he insists on having no emotional connection with Ana. But she tells him that sex isn't enough. She wants more.

The story reminded me of *Pretty Woman,* when Julia Roberts says to Richard Gere, "No kissing." The implication is that kissing or touching (thanks to oxytocin) results in emotional connection, and both Christian Grey and the *Pretty Woman* character want to avoid that. At first. Eventually, of course, they both give in—otherwise there'd be no love story.

Unfortunately, American women live in a culture that *ignores* human nature. In response to the recent development that women in America make up the majority of the workforce, Liza Mundy wrote in *The Richer Sex: How the New Majority of Female Breadwinners Is Transforming Sex, Love, and Family,* that the traditional family is dead—and that human behavior must change to reflect this fact. "The rise of women earners will shape human behavior by challenging some of the most primal and hardwired ways men and women see one another. It will alter how we mate, how and when we join together, how we procreate and raise children, and how we pursue happiness. It will reshape the landscape of the heart."[4]

What feminists envision is an androgynous world. They want men and women to be virtually indistinguishable—that's why they love the LGBT community, where gender is murky or skewed. The rest of America, meanwhile, like and want traditional families. Or just *some form* of a traditional family. It doesn't have to be *Leave It to Beaver*—mine isn't. But the basic structure is the same.

I don't pretend it will be easy to find what you're looking for. I saw a clip on the *Today Show* about Olympic athlete Lolo Jones. She's thirty years old, gorgeous, and a proud virgin. Apparently Lolo had a series of obstacles to overcome in life. She attended eight different schools in an eight-year period while her single mother, Lori, sometimes held two jobs to support her family of six. Lolo's father spent most of her childhood either in the Air Force or in state prison. When Lolo was in the third grade, her family settled in the basement of a Salvation Army church.

To cope, Lolo did two things. One, she concentrated all her energies on track, with the goal of winning an Olympic medal. Two, she committed herself to virginity. Lolo knew that in order to achieve her dreams, both professionally and personally (she wants a normal, traditional family like most women do), she would need to keep herself on the straight and narrow. She needed to stay focused—and she did.

The downside is that it's been hard for Lolo to find a great guy. As I said at the beginning of the book, guys tend to go where they can get some action. It has always been this way. Today, unfortunately, the "action" is everywhere—which makes finding a husband really hard for women like Lolo Jones.

Women like her are the kind of role models young women lack. All we see today see are women who tout the feminist agenda: they sleep around, are self-absorbed, and are mired in victimhood. If Lolo had chosen to remain a victim of her circumstances—and she certainly could have—she would not be where she is today. Lolo Jones is a great example of true female empowerment.

But don't mistake being empowered with being employed. Yes, making money is *one* way to feel empowered. But it's not the only way. According to the *Free Online Dictionary*, to *empower* means simply "to equip or supply with an ability; to enable."[5]

The word *empowerment* has been butchered. It's associated almost exclusively with female independence, as though a woman who can stand on her own and never depend on a man is the arbiter of empowerment. Look at how the press handled the Tom Cruise and Katie Holmes split (although you could think of any celebrity split, really). The headlines routinely referred to Katie's newfound "freedom," as though getting divorced and becoming a single mom is a positive, ennobling thing. They even called her a "feminist hero." Just as we never see what happens *after* the end of a Hollywood movie, we never hear about what happens after the divorce is final. By then the magazines have moved on to something else.

The obvious impression left in people's minds is that women are better off without men. Women assume that what their mothers told them about never relying on a man was smart. But has women's new economic empowerment enabled women to leave bad marriages? Or has it provided so much wiggle room that women can easily get out of *all* marriages, good or bad? Because when high-profile women walk away from a bad marriage, the assumption is always that the woman is the wronged spouse. No other scenario is entertained.

There really is a whole different way to view money in a marriage. Of course it's great for women to get college educations and compete in the marketplace. But there's going to come a time in every woman's life when she will need to, and most likely want to, be liberated from producing an income. This doesn't make her inferior in *any* way, and she shouldn't feel that way. As Eleanor Roosevelt said, "No one can make you feel inferior without your consent."[6] Leaving one's husband and becoming a single mother is not the least bit empowering. It's sad. Lonely. Depressing. And terrible for the kids.

The headlines skip over that part.

Here's a twist. Why not view money as the glue that holds a family together? It's true that if you're married to one of the bad guys, dependence is a bad thing. But remember: this book doesn't speak to that group. Plus the "bad guy" scenario has been greatly exaggerated. The assumption that husbands dump their wives at the slightest provocation (which statistically isn't even accurate: as mentioned earlier, two-thirds of all divorces are initiated by women) is harmful to the institution of marriage and to society as a whole.

When it comes to money and marriage, women will do themselves a favor by doing three things. One: assume the best, not the worst, of your guy. Two: support your husband in his career goals. His work life will be far more linear than yours. This means when you're dating, your guy should not be following you all over the country according to *your* career plans. If it works to do so because his career is flexible, fine. But he should not be changing his course of action to suit your plans, since your plans will likely change once you become a mother.

Don't use the money you've made as leverage, freeing yourself from what very well may be a salvageable marriage. Certainly if you find yourself married to a bum, money will allow you to escape. But don't rest on your laurels. It's too easy to stop working on your marriage when you know you can cut and run.

That's also a good reason to join bank accounts, by the way. Like taking your husband's name, having a joint bank account tells your husband you're in this thing all the way. Many wives assume that not joining bank accounts makes them less vulnerable to divorce. They think of it in the same way they think of cohabitation: as insurance against future doom and gloom. In reality, separate bank accounts create a self-fulfilling prophecy. It starts everything out on a negative note and is therefore more likely to end badly. Not always, but often.

Why take the gamble?

*Step #8*

# KNOW YOUR BODY

A TRAGEDY HAS BEFALLEN AMERICAN WOMEN—and no, it's not the struggle to find so-called balance. Few other modern crises have been as financially and emotionally devastating as an entire generation of women discovering they're physically unable to have children.

The most egregious aspect of this phenomenon is that, for many women, the circumstances are almost entirely preventable. But the truth about fertility has been squelched. No one wants to say to women, "You have a window, ladies. Wait too long, and you'll be sorry." So I'll say it.

Ladies: you have a window. Wait too long, and you'll be sorry.

Here's some sobering news: According to the Human Fertilisation and Embryology Authority, which collects data on roughly fifty thousand fertility treatments performed each year in the UK, nearly *a quarter* of the patients who sought treatments in order to become pregnant (between 1991 and 2008, the average age of the study's patients was 35) experienced "Unexplained Infertility."[1] "Male factors" was a bit higher, at 29.7 percent. But *all* the other data as to why women couldn't conceive—ovarian failure, endometriosis, etc.—paled in comparison to "Unexplained Infertility." But there's nothing inexplicable about it. The reason these women can't conceive is because they waited too long.

Mother Nature is a powerful force. If she had her way, most women would become mothers in their teens. (Yikes! Let's not do that . . .) But

Mother Nature closes the window too. "The likelihood of getting pregnant following IVF or DI treatment is strongly linked to the age of the woman being treated. On average, a woman under thirty-five years old is substantially more likely to conceive than a woman who is older."[2] Once you're over forty, it's nearly impossible—at least without serious and expensive medical intervention.

This seems like basic information women need, don't you think? Yet even doctors won't relay this data. Imagine looking into the eyes of a thirty-nine-year-old woman who's praying for a baby and telling her she's waited too long to conceive. Not gonna happen.

Take Kate, who happens to be someone I know, but there's nothing unusual about her story. Kate took years to get to the altar. Not because she didn't have a boyfriend—she did—but because she was uber-focused on her career. Like so many young women, Kate stayed in school for almost a *decade* as she bounced around from one career concept to another. At thirty-two, she decided to marry her longtime boyfriend. Then she waited another three years to start talking about having kids. Just talking, mind you.

That's when things went south. By the time Kate and her husband got down to business, her body didn't want to cooperate. Kate had several miscarriages. Despondent, she visited her doctor, who told her getting pregnant was not going to be easy. So Kate began fertility treatments. It took five treatments, and thirty thousand dollars, to get one baby. One. When he was born, Kate was thirty-eight. Desperate for another baby, she and her husband depleted their savings account to try to make it happen. It never did.

Same thing happened to Rebecca Walker, daughter of Alice Walker, who wrote *The Color Purple*. Rebecca wrote a compelling article detailing her unfortunate feminist upbringing. Here's a portion of it:

> As a child, I yearned for a traditional mother. . . . I grew up believing that children are millstones around your neck and the idea that motherhood can make you happy is a complete fairy tale. . . . When I hit my 20s, . . . I could feel my biological clock ticking, but I felt if I listened to it, I would be betraying my mother and all she had taught me. . . . In fact, having a child has been the most rewarding experience of my life. . . . My only regret is that I discovered the joys of motherhood so late—I have been trying for a second child, but so far with no luck.[3]

Now, to be fair, most women didn't grow up with feminist mothers as strident as Alice Walker. But they did grow up with mothers who implied that marriage and motherhood hold women back. Either that, or they *did* have traditional mothers but let the culture steer them wrong.

Regardless of the reason, there's so much you need to know about infertility. Let's begin with the research compiled by Miriam Grossman, MD, a former campus psychiatrist at UCLA. Out of concern for the scores of college girls who showed up at her door for advice about sex and STDs, Grossman designed a pamphlet called *Sense & Sexuality*. Here's the part on fertility:

> Seventy-five percent of college freshmen say raising a family is an "essential or very important goal." Yet 55% of younger high-achieving women are childless at thirty-five, and 89% think they'll be able to get pregnant into their forties. This is patently false.
>
> It is easiest for a woman to conceive and deliver a healthy child in her twenties. Fertility declines slightly at thirty, and more dramatically at thirty-five. Waiting rooms of fertility clinics are packed with health-conscious women who work out and count calories—they're there because they're forty years old.[4]

Prior to the 1960s, women didn't need facts like these because most women had children in their twenties. Then feminists came along and told women to pursue a career and delay motherhood as long as possible. But women's progress outside the home has meant *regress* for women inside the home. Some things in life we can't change, and our fertility is one of them. We cannot make our bodies do what we want them to do.

Don't misunderstand. I'm not saying delayed childbirth is a terrible idea in and of itself. Personally, I think the ideal age to have a child is thirty (or late twenties if you want a larger family.) But if women *are* going to delay motherhood, they need to know the facts—and most don't. All they see are high-profile women who have babies much later in life. These actresses and television personalities—women like Susan Sarandon, Brooke Shields, Geena Davis, Salma Hayek, Mariska Hargitay, Nicole Kidman, and Kelly Preston—help foster the notion, perhaps unwittingly, that motherhood can be chosen in whatever manner and on whatever timetable women choose.

It doesn't work that way. The only reason these women can do it is because they have a bottomless pit of cash to force the issue via a petri dish. That's why it was a breath of fresh air to read *Desperate Housewives'* Marcia Cross tell *People* magazine that having babies later in life is "like a miracle." She added, "What I didn't want to do was put out the myth that you can be in your forties and just pop out kids . . . It's very, very difficult to get pregnant in your 40s. It's costly and tough on your body and your relationship."[5]

Brooke Shields has been honest as well. "It's important for women to be aware of potential problems and to take control. Two eggs do not an omelette make."[6] And Courteney Cox: "I get pregnant pretty easily, but I have a hard time keeping them."[7]

Kudos to these ladies for telling the truth—really, that's what every celebrity who becomes a mother at a late age should do. These women have a moral obligation to set the record straight; it's one of the trade-offs for being so revered in our Hollywood-obsessed culture. Unfortunately, comments like theirs get lost in the shuffle. Salma Hayek's claim that "there's no reason women should feel rushed to have a child"[8] is far more commonplace. And it's destructive.

I know the choice to delay motherhood feels liberating: it frees you up to do other things. But remember when I said too much choice can be counterproductive? Twenty-something blogger, Kate Fridkis, who's married but does not have children yet, is a great illustration of just how gut-wrenching choice has become. In an article titled "The Invisible Baby That Follows Me Around," she wrote:

> People ask me, "So are you guys thinking about kids?" That's what happens when you get married. Even in New York City, the land of not-having-to-think-about-kids-until-you're-30. "I think I'll have a baby when I'm thirty, man or not," said one of my friends at a group event. "What?" the other twenty-something women cried. "Thirty? That's too young! How about thirty-five?" The land of not-having-to-think-about-kids-until-you're-35.
>
>     The thing is—I want to have a baby. Sometimes I want to have one RIGHT NOW. I'm a little embarrassed to admit that. Especially since people from NYC read this blog. Sometimes I see a baby and I get that melty feeling that women get when they fit scientifically

supported stereotypes. It's like my uterus is talking to me. It's sort of sly and purring. "Come on . . . you know you want one . . . you could have one . . ." And then I go home and stare at the wreckage of the book I'm trying to write, and I feel slightly panicky. And then my brain turns to steel and snaps at my uterus to please be quiet until you have something worthwhile to say. I have things to do. Lots of things. I have to make something of myself.

That damn clock.[9]

Then Fridkis added this nugget of wisdom: "In the world I live in, 'making something of yourself' means your career. In my mom's world, it means your family. This is all very confusing." Translation: America's values are so screwed up that Ms. Fridkis (and she's certainly not alone) feels she must justify her existence by being employed. That's what I mean when I say the culture is against you.

Bottom line: know your body. You do have some time, but you don't have all the time in the world. If you wait too long, you will feel rushed—and that can make it harder to conceive. (It can also mean making a poor choice of husband.) I've heard so many stories about women who tried desperately to get pregnant, only to end up adopting because they thought they couldn't get pregnant, and then—wham!—they got pregnant. Our bodies don't perform on command.

That's why it's best to start thinking in your twenties about when you want children. You don't have to *do* anything about it—you just need to be thinking about it, as opposed to living day by day and giving it no thought whatsoever because you think you're invincible. When it comes to having babies, there's a window. And that window isn't just about the ability to conceive; it's about the ability to conceive a healthy child. The older women are, the more likely they are to have a child with Down syndrome. And just recently, researchers in Iceland found that older fathers transmit more genetic mutations—such as schizophrenia and autism—to their offspring, and this effect grows with each year of age.

The good news is, there's no cap on women's desire to accomplish most of what they want out of life. Women today have fewer children than ever and simultaneously live longer lives. You just can't do everything all at once. The key is to think long-term. Do *not* live in the moment. Think. Plan. Prepare. Decide.

And when things don't go exactly as planned (and they won't), be flexible. Reorganize and regroup. Do what you need to do. But always, always have a plan. Living moment to moment is what causes so many women to wake up one day and realize their window to conceive, or even get married, came and went. They thought they had all the time in the world. They didn't. You don't either.

*Step #9*

# ACCEPT IT:
# YOU CAN'T HAVE IT ALL

S O NOW WE'VE ARRIVED at the *number one* issue for women when it comes to getting married and settling down: how to "balance" work and family. This is a subject close to my heart, and I can't stand the way the media handles it. Whenever they address the subject of working mothers, it's almost always framed in the context of balance.

*Balance* is the wrong word. The word *balance* means a state of equilibrium, or an equal distribution of weight. It refers to emotional stability, calm behavior and judgment, etc. I can assure you none of these meanings comes close to describing what it's like to "balance" work and family.

When mothers work outside the home, the distribution of weight is never even, and emotions often run high. Where do you think the concept of mommy guilt came from? Or how about women's stress? These terms are new in relation to motherhood. They exist as a result of women trying to care for children, particularly young children, while *at the same time* pursuing demanding careers. "It's just like any working mom's dilemma. It's tough. It's a balancing act. You put them first and then you have all these other things you have to do, things you have to give your time to as well, and you have to make sure they're okay in the process," Jennifer Lopez responded when asked why she left *American Idol*.[1]

You need to understand something very important that the media are never going to tell you. If you attempt to raise children while working full-time and year-round, guilt will never stop tormenting you. That's your serotonin talking. No man, employer, or poorly designed government is keeping you from balancing work and family. If you want to be mad about it, take your issue up with God.

That's *never* how the issue is framed in the media. If you read women's magazines, you'll find scores of articles devoted to helping mothers try to alleviate their guilt, justify their guilt, or get rid of their guilt. Yes, mothers of every era have felt stabs of guilt for no good reason. But "mommy guilt" is a new phenomenon. Ever since the mass exodus of mothers from the home, guilt has become a major part of women's lives. That's because if you're not there to take care of your children most of their waking hours, you are going to feel bad about it. It's not any more complicated than that.

Which brings me to this question: Why do it to yourself if you don't have to? Mothering is hard enough without the guilt. The only way to avoid the kind of debilitating guilt that eats women alive is to not try and do everything and be everything all at once. Women must stop living their lives as if they're going to die tomorrow and won't be able to get everything done. There's plenty of time. Relax.

This might sound silly, but let's compare your life to ordering a meal at a restaurant. When you sit down, everything on the menu looks great: the steak, the scallops, the salmon. Your mouth is salivating over all the options. And while in reality you could order it all, you'd be too full to enjoy the whole thing. You'd only get to experience bits and pieces of each. And who wants just three bites of a fifty-dollar steak?

So what can you do? Order one meal one night, and come back another night to try the next one. It's as simple as that. You make a choice, and you make the most of it. Making choices is part of life. You can't go to every party. You can't go on every vacation. You can't go to every college. You have to choose.

Most married mothers who work full-time outside the home are making a choice. They are *choosing* to focus the bulk of their time and attention on their jobs, as opposed to on their homes and their children. They're not balancing anything—they're performing a juggling act. Jugglers never have both or all of the balls in the air at one time. When one is up, the other is down. To juggle means "to alternately toss and catch something," or "to have difficulty holding more than one thing at a time."

That's the opposite of balance.

Ironically, to juggle (according to Merriam-Webster) also means "to practice deception," or "to manipulate in order to deceive." In my last book, *The Flipside of Feminism*, I devoted an entire chapter to the argument that multitasking is a fraud and referred to a great book called *The Myth of Multitasking*. The message of this book is that the human brain is like a computer: it is capable of focusing on only one thing at a time. Switching back and forth between different tasks cannot overcome the brain's inability to process two sets of data simultaneously. Thus, multitasking is a myth.

I'm not saying you can't do *any* two things at once. You may, for example, be able to put dinner together while helping your second grader with homework. But the fancier the recipe and more complicated the homework, the less successful you will be at either one. Juggling two or more activities that require mental acuity is not the same as doing laundry and talking on the phone. And I've even messed that up. (My particular favorite is watching people grocery shop while having a conversation with their friends on their iPhones. The few times I've attempted this, I invariably returned home with the wrong items.)

Mothers who work full-time and have children at home, particularly young children, are simply doing two things at once, half as well. They are becoming jacks-of-all-trades and masters of none, which is why they're so guilt-ridden and stressed out all the time. It's also the reason why, historically, women have waited until their children were older and more independent before taking outside jobs.

And even *that's* not the same as being employed once children have left home. When that happens, the whole world opens up to women. I don't know about you, but I don't plan to hang up my hat when my kids graduate from high school. A woman's life has seasons: a time for this, and a time for that. The problem is that the modern generation wants everything *right now*.

For years I've been banging the pot loudly about how important it is to be there for one's children and how impossible it is to have it all at one time. And every time I do, people want to know how I manage my own life. Or, if they're mad at my message—which is often the case—they'll tell me I'm a hypocrite.

Here I am, they say, a woman who clearly has it all. Yet I insist having it all isn't possible. I tell other women they should stay home, they say; yet I traipse all over the country, giving speeches, or I sit at my computer all day while my children fend for themselves. These folks imagine a gotcha moment: *Aha!* they think. *Suzanne must have a well-paid nanny in the background. Either that, or there's some other secret she's not sharing. Maybe her kids have been raised on the idiot box, or her mother raised her kids for her. Something's not right.*

The reason people make these assumptions is twofold. One, they assume I *do* have it all—which I don't. My writing career is exactly half of what it could be if I did not have a husband and children. (And that's as it should be.) Two, things are never as they appear—hence, the assumptions.

My argument has always been the same. Women who are looking to combine work and family should make clear and purposeful choices with this goal in mind, or structure their lives in such a way that they can make it happen. They must also recognize that children have needs, and these needs must be met. The reason women struggle with this is once again twofold.

For one thing, the average woman today gives no thought to marriage and motherhood when she's young. Instead, she maps out her life according to her big career plans and lets the chips fall where they may when it comes to the rest. Two, "having it all," to many women, doesn't mean having a little of this and a little of that—the way it does to me. It means being able to accomplish *anything they want, to any degree they desire*, while still maintaining a normal, healthy family life. That's impossible. Literally: it's impossible. No one can do this. No one has yet.

Why should you be any different?

The women in your life lied to you. You can't *really* do or be anything you want if you plan to get married and have children. In my first book, which I published more than ten years ago, I wrote exactly that: "The fact remains that some careers just won't be an option for women—particularly the powerful and lucrative ones. We can choose them, if we wish; but not without ramifications. What's difficult about this is that it flies in the face of feminism. That is, women can't really do or be whatever they want because of sheer biology. Becoming a doctor or big-shot attorney will inevitably pose a problem for women who plan to have children."[2]

This was the crux of the hoopla surrounding the article in *The Atlantic* entitled "Why Women Can't Have It All." The author, Anne-Marie Slaughter, pointed out what I've been hammering home for years: women can't have it all. Life is about trade-offs. And my life is certainly no different.

I realize it doesn't look that way from the outside. After all, people see me on TV or hear me on the radio and assume I have some highfalutin career. I also do speaking engagements on occasion, so the assumption is that I'm routinely flying all over the country (or world). I was interviewed recently, and one of the hosts opened the segment saying, "So you travel the country talking about . . ."

So let's begin there. I *do not* "travel the country." My speaking engagements, as well as TV spots, are few and far between—they are not the bulk of what I do. They also require only between a few hours and one day to accomplish. The main thing I do when I'm not busy being a mom is write.

Writing happens to be a career I can control: I work from home; I'm not at the mercy of a boss; I can say no to anything that conflicts with my personal life; and I can work my entire schedule around my children's needs. So while on paper I'm what people call a "working mother," I'm a terrible example of one. Because of *very purposeful choices* I've made along the way, I have been my children's sole caregiver from sunrise to dinnertime, all week long. I even have the tax returns to prove it.

I recognize, of course, that not everyone can work from home and that in this way I'm fortunate. However, becoming a writer was not my original plan. I was going to, and did, become a teacher. But I ultimately decided even that career, for me, would conflict with motherhood. That's because if I'm going to do something, I can't do it halfway. For me, teaching was as all consuming as being a lawyer or doctor. So I changed course.

I made other choices as well. I have two children instead of four, though that was partly because I had my second child at thirty-five. Still, I *could* have tried for a third. I also divorced one man who I feared would not be around much and married a man whose career goals were less extreme and who is therefore more available as a hands-on dad. *Do not underestimate any of these choices.* The number of children you want, the kind of man you marry, and the type of work you choose to do are all critical factors in your ability to "have it all."

That said, *having it all* is really the wrong phrase—perhaps even the wrong goal. If by "having it all" you mean that over the course of your lifetime you will have accomplished more than one thing, great. But you can't be president, or fly to the moon, or even make it to the corner office if being a hands-on, get-your-hands-dirty kind of mother is nonnegotiable. For me, it was. It is.

Bottom line: How visible I am as a writer and speaker at any given time depends entirely on where my children are in their development, both physically and emotionally. When they were babies and toddlers, I dropped out of sight completely. When they are grown and gone, I expect to up the ante.

If you look at the past thirteen years of my life, the times I've actually "worked" have almost always been when my kids were asleep, at school, or otherwise engaged. I've never employed a nanny; my children never went to daycare (in fact, they started school late by today's standards); and I've never had family help of any consequence. My mother is older than most of my friends' mothers, so her ability to be physically engaged with my children was limited.

I do have a leg up, however, in that my husband works from home. And while that is a strain in its own way (indeed, I wouldn't recommend it!), it has unquestionably allowed me to pursue my writing career more easily. I simply could not do what I do without two things: my husband's steady, reliable income, and the flexibility of both our jobs. Whom you choose to marry really does matter.

If you want to be successful at home and at work, start with this premise: *you've been sold a script for your life that isn't going to work.* The most important thing you need to know going forward is that as long as you have some form of employment on your plate when you have children, you will never feel fully relaxed—or, in some cases, even content. That's just the way it is; and you should not blame your husband, your employer, or the government for this predicament. If you don't want to feel this way, don't attempt to work outside the home at all when you have children. Though the media would like you to believe otherwise, there are millions of women who choose this path.

If you don't have children, imagine what a Sunday with them would look like. Imagine how the day would unfold and what the climate in the home would be like. Now compare that to an average workday when both parents are employed full-time and what those days must look and feel like. Actually, let me tell you what it feels like since I've experienced it a time or two when I've had a deadline: crappy.

When you remove the work-related task from the equation, when you focus exclusively on the needs of your children and the home, *which are going to take up a considerable portion of your time no matter how you organize your time*, your attitude toward motherhood is welcomed rather than resented. You're just a whole different kind of mother when you don't have someplace you need to be, or something else you need to get done. The only way to feel good about performing a task—whether it's work-related or home-related—is to give it your undivided attention.

I assume you'd rather enjoy your children than resent them. If so, throw the concept of having it all in the trash, where it belongs. Create realistic expectations for what you can accomplish while you're raising children, and find a job or career that's flexible. If you absolutely can't find anything that works, let it go. Don't work. "Work" can bring great benefits at the right time of your life, but it shouldn't be your raison d'être. Don't get overly invested in anything other than your family.

When people look at my life, some assume I lucked out, that it all just "happened." That isn't the case. Most women didn't do what I did. They were too busy living day to day, or they succumbed to the culture's message that women should focus solely on their careers. As a result, many end up at the mercy of their jobs. They made choices based on the assumption that they'd always be in the workforce. I didn't do that.

When both parents try to bring home a paycheck *and* plan for, prepare, and cook seven days' worth of meals every week; do the dishes; pay the bills; mow the lawn; paint the shutters; fix the leaky faucet; go to Target; do the laundry; pick up the dry cleaning; take out the trash (on the right day at the right time so it doesn't get backed up and stink up your house and garage); go to Home Depot; shop for clothes; take the kids to the doctor; return phone calls; maintain their friendships; go to the gym . . . oh, and raise helpless babies to become healthy, mature, responsible adults, the result can be only chaos. People can spin it any way they want, but chaos is chaos.

Raising children and maintaining a home were never meant to be sideline occupations. The only reason Americans don't look at it this way is because our views on parenting have changed. We're too focused on what adults want rather than what children need.

Remember when I talked about the 1960s cultural shift away from the universal moral order and onto moral relativity, or doing what's best for the individual? The mass exodus of mothers from the home is a quintessential example of this phenomenon. The universal moral order demanded people do what's best for the family. With moral relativity firmly in place, the knee-jerk reaction to working motherhood is indifference. The decision about whether or not to stay home and raise one's children is viewed as no different from the choice between vanilla or chocolate.

When a pregnant Melissa Mayer was named the new Yahoo CEO, scores of articles were written about it. The theme was that society shouldn't have any opinion about the fact that Mayer says she won't need maternity leave. That would be judgmental, and making value judgments is the ultimate taboo in modern America.

But Ms. Mayer's decision to give birth and then return to her former life as though nothing happened would have been a shocking action, let alone thought, prior to the feminist movement. Our mothers and grandmothers didn't have the burden of "deciding" whether or not they wanted to stay home with their children. It was assumed they would. It was understood that giving birth is the *least* of a mother's job, that what comes afterward is what really matters.

There are two ways to view this monumental cultural shift: as a boon for women's "choice," or as a tragedy for children, families, and society as a whole.

Since the culture makes it clear that the former view is the correct one, it makes sense that mothers who are on the fence about whether or not to stay home would need some incentive to make that choice. They need to understand *why* it's important to do so. Other women know they want to stay home but need to convince their boyfriends or husbands it's the right thing to do. That's how destructive feminism has been.

If you do run into this problem, here's what you tell your guy. First, contrary to popular belief, it is *not* economically sound for both parents to work full-time—at least when children are young. Two, the needs of children, especially babies, are not being met. As Dr. William Sears wrote in *The Baby Book*, "Some mothers choose to go back to their jobs simply because they don't understand how disruptive that is to the well being of their babies."[3]

A lot of parents think babies just sit there like lumps. They think nothing of any consequence happens until children are older. That isn't true. The early years are critical for bonding.

We don't hear much about bonding, yet it's vital not only to our children's health but to the health of our nation. Bonding is how human beings develop traits such as trust, empathy, compassion, and intimacy. These aren't traits we're born with, like personality traits. They're learned.

In the first three years.

Accepting this is a tall order for Americans who've been conditioned to embrace daycare, but we ignore this fact at our peril. When babies fail to bond, it's bad news for all of us. The loss of self-worth these individuals experience from having been either ignored or passed around from caregiver to caregiver stays with them for life. When babies don't have one primary caregiver, preferably but not necessarily the mother, who tends to the baby the majority of his or her waking hours, babies run the risk of failing to bond. "Young children do not form a strong attachment to a person they see little of, no matter how kindly the person is or how superlative the quality of time spent together," wrote William and Wendy Dreskin, coauthors of *The Day Care Decision* and former owners/directors of a daycare center.[4]

Indeed, parents need to be physically and emotionally available to their children if they expect to do the job well. That's not *all* there is to it, but it's a definite prerequisite. When babies are separated for long periods of time from their mothers or alternate primary caregiver, they may never learn how to trust or love.

This is a delicate subject, to say the least. It's one of those topics we're not supposed to talk about so that parents who use daycare (or hire come-and-go nannies) won't feel bad. But there's so much misinformation about daycare, or child care in general. The main thing you need to know is this: substitute care for children, even babies, isn't harmful *when used sparingly*. It's the every-day, all-day substitute care that's the problem.

By "sparingly," I mean a few hours here and there, the same way you might leave a baby or toddler at home with a sitter. Three days a week at a child care center, from eight to five, does not constitute "sparingly." A baby who attends daycare five days a week for three hours a day is actually better off than the baby who attends daycare three days a week from eight to five. That's because it's *the number of hours at one time* that matter. It's just too disruptive to babies' sleep and food schedules, and to the bonding process.

There's tons of information about this subject, if you're interested— it's fascinating stuff. I first studied it in college. Boston University had an accredited daycare in its school of education, and I would go behind one of those windows where the toddlers couldn't see me but I could see them, and I would study their interactions with their mothers when they dropped them off.

I also worked in numerous childcare environments and as a nanny during the summers. But it wasn't until I became a mother and wrote my first book, *7 Myths of Working Mothers* (which was essentially about the needs of children) that I became passionate about the issue. I wish all parents were privy to the information. If they were, I think they'd make very different choices about their child care arrangements.

Just to be clear, I'm not suggesting mothers should never leave their babies in other people's care. This isn't about mom and baby being joined at the hip—I'm not a spokesperson for attachment parenting. What I *am* saying is that if you disappear from your baby's view every day, all day—or even most of the day—he will bond with the person in whose care you left him. Babies attach themselves to whomever they see the most of. You've probably heard about working mothers who become jealous of their nannies. That's why.

I'm also not suggesting daycare shouldn't exist. But by opening it up to anyone who wants to use it, by having it become a *way of life*, it fails to be effective. The quality of daycare matters, yes. But quality can exist only when the supply exceeds the demand. Right now we have the reverse. No large-scale bureaucratic system can possibly do for children what parents have historically done for free. It's impossible.

This is an uncomfortable truth, to be sure. And the reason you don't know about the perils of daycare is because the media won't report it, or even acknowledge it. As Bernard Goldberg pointed out in his book *Bias*, the women in the media drop their children off with someone else for twelve or more hours a day, every day—they're hardly in a position to be objective. Facing this subject would make them feel bad. Which means unless you have firsthand experience working with babies and toddlers or have a degree in child development, unless you've researched the issue ad nauseam, unless you've stayed home with your children and really paid attention to the bonding process, there's no way you'd know any of this.

I'm not telling you this to make you feel guilty should you decide to put your children in daycare. I'm telling you this because I don't want you to have regrets. Embracing the cultural trend regarding motherhood, the one that says, "Take a short break and then get back to the office," means giving something up you cannot get back. You have one chance—one—to be with your children in the early years, not just for the sake of bonding, but for your own joy and satisfaction as well.

So let's get back to the burning question, the one every woman wants to know: How can women combine the needs of children, and their desire to be with them, with their hunger for an independent life?

Depends. How many children do you want? Because the more children you have, the longer it will be before you feel comfortable turning your attention away from home. Second, what do you want your independent life to consist of? If a career is the goal, the only way to do it *without feeling stressed or guilty, without living in chaos,* and *without suffering from a gnawing sense that nothing you're doing is being done well* is to (a) sequence your life, or look at your life as one long journey in which you'll have plenty of time to do both things—but at separate times; (b) marry the right guy; and (c) choose a flexible career. If you choose a career that takes you away from home most of your children's waking hours, you're going to be unhappy. That's all there is to it.

Let's look at Oprah Winfrey a sec. Here's a woman whose professional goals were so high the only way for her to achieve them was to give up marriage and motherhood altogether. Sugar Rautbord, a fellow Chicagoan who knew Oprah long before she became a millionaire media mogul, told biographer Kitty Kelley, "[Oprah] figured out early that the only way to have a successful career and make money—big money—was to delete husbands and children and carpools from life's agenda."[5] Oprah Winfrey eats, sleeps, and breathes work—there's very little time for anything else. That is how you reach those heights.

Any woman who wants that kind of life is free to go and get it. But when most women think honestly about their lives, a solitary life vacant of family—not to mention all the other facets of life that get lost in the shuffle (exercise, friendships, cooking, free time, etc.)—is not what they want. This is a sore point for the feminist elite, who insist women make less money than men due to workplace discrimination. The truth, of course, is that most women choose to make family the focus of their lives. Unlike the feminist elite, most women's careers are not the reason they get up every morning. *That's* why they make less money than men.

Keep in mind the media will say that if you don't start working at twenty-two and not stop until you're sixty-five—you know: like men do—that you'll be at a disadvantage. But of course, that depends how you view being "disadvantaged." If your life's focus is your career and that's how you measure success, then yes, you'll be at a disadvantage. If, however, your definition of success includes being a fully engaged wife, mother, friend, daughter, etc., well then, you're not at a disadvantage at all, are you?

The good news is that it's much easier for women to sequence their lives today. Technological advances provide enormous flexibility, allowing women to work from home or keep themselves engaged in the world outside their doorstep. Many women (many *people*) also find that whatever path they embarked upon in their twenties doesn't interest them down the road.

I can't tell you how important it is that you marry a man who understands this stuff—because those who've fallen for feminist dogma, even unknowingly, have a different take on work and family "balance." As I already mentioned, men have been just as conditioned as women to believe babies don't need their mothers. Moreover, the culture insists that children whose mothers don't like staying home are better off in daycare.

That's simply not true. As renowned psychiatrist John Bowlby once said, "A home must be very bad before it can be bettered by a good institution."[6] Children in low-income families, where stability is lacking or drugs are rampant, is one thing. A middle-class family with a mom and a dad in which the mother is simply bored is something else. Children don't care if their mothers are happy or self-actualized. They just want them around.

(By the way, I feel compelled to point out that one of the reasons at-home motherhood has become "boring" for some is precisely *because* so many mothers have left home for the workplace. Had they not, raising babies and toddlers would not be so taxing. Women would have other mothers around to help them and to provide some much-needed comic relief. That's the real meaning of the phrase "it takes a village.")

It has been my observation that most women decide—even if it takes them years to figure it out—that they want marriage and motherhood to be the center of their lives. When you're young, you don't have babies on your mind. I get that. But because you live in a culture that assumes you can't, or won't want to, stay home when the time comes—which is a complete reverse of the way things used to be for women—you have to be able to think outside the box. You have to ask yourself in advance, when you're in college, what it is that you really want out of life.

You'll also have to ignore your professors, most of whom are feminist thinkers. Universities are supposed to be genuinely liberal, or open to all schools of thought. But they're not. They preach leftist politics all day long, and the most popular branch is feminism. The more prestigious the school, the more pronounced the feminism.

Which means just when women are mapping out their futures, they're saturated with feminist propaganda. Rather than get the kind of guidance I'm giving you, which incorporates *all* the different aspects of a woman's life—health, work, friendships, children, a husband, free time—women get the singular message that their careers will, and should, be the focus of their lives. This is a philosophy most women come to regret.

In 2007, the National Bureau of Economic Research released this finding: "As women have gained more freedom, more education, and more power, they have become less happy."[7] While the authors are careful not to blame feminism directly, they did write this: "As women's expectations move into alignment with their experiences, this decline in happiness may reverse."[8] Why did women's expectations change in the first place? You got it: feminism.

Here's a great example of the message college students absorb. In 2011, one of the most powerful women in America, Facebook COO Sheryl Sandberg, delivered the commencement address at Barnard College, an all-girls school. During her speech, she offered the graduates the typical feminist/self-esteem message: that there's an amazing world out there, just waiting for women to make their mark. She told the graduates they should stop at nothing to achieve their dreams. There was no mention of what these young women's futures will really look like: no talk of husbands or children; no talk of how their priorities will change; no talk of anything but their bombastic future careers.

Then Sandberg chimed in with her larger message regarding social change. She assured the graduates that women have a long way to go to achieve "equality" and offered her vision for America. "A world where men ran half our homes and women ran half our institutions would be just a much better world," she said. She prefaced this by saying, "To solve this generation's central moral problem, which is gender equality[,] [w]e need women at all levels, including the top, to change the dynamic, reshape the conversation, to make sure women's voices are heard and heeded, not overlooked and ignored."[9]

Putting aside for a moment Sandberg's shocking assertion that America's *central moral problem* is gender equality, she also told the graduates to think big. "Do not leave before you leave. Do not lean back; lean in. Put your foot on that gas pedal and keep it there until the day you have to make a decision."[10] The day she's referring to, of course, is the day women decide to opt out of the workforce to have children.

That there aren't more women like Sandberg—women who choose to keep their foot on the pedal and pay other women to raise their children so they *can* keep their foot on the pedal—riles feminists. Women like Sandberg are personally vested in getting other women on board. If feminists are successful, they get the reassurance they need that the choices they've made are right, normal, and even good. Feminists are very insecure about their feminine proclivities (or lack thereof). Thus, they're desperate for validation.

But Sheryl Sandberg is not your typical high-profile feminist. She's not single, divorced, or gay. She is married with two young children, and she admits to feeling guilty being away from home. "I feel guilty working because of my kids. I do. I feel guilty," she announced at a TED conference.[11] At one point she glossed over what it's like to have her toddler son pulling on his mother's leg, begging her not to go to work—as if that's something women should just get over.

That tugging is the perfect metaphor for the greater tug women feel between their independent selves and their nurturing selves. Very few women are immune to it. But rather than address this conflict head-on, women like Sandberg encourage women to ignore their nurturing side and dismiss their children's needs.

I'm encouraging you to do the opposite.

Sandberg's directive does introduce a bigger question, though—one with which so many Americans, not just women, grapple: What is success? I truly believe most people know success is not something one deposits in a bank. Unless they lack any semblance of spirituality, people know we're here on this earth not for the money we make or the fame we achieve. We're here for the relationships we build. That's why marrying a man who's on your side when it comes to the work/life dilemma—whether and how much to work outside the home once children come along—cannot be underestimated. It can make or break your marriage.

At the very least, you need to know that mothering is hard. More than hard—it will rock your world. The last thing you need as a mother, particularly a new mother, is the added stress of a dual-income lifestyle. Motherhood can be joyous, but only if you aren't rushing off someplace all the time. The moment you're in a rush, the resentment starts to build. Don't let it. Iris Krasnow said it best in *Surrendering to Motherhood*: "Don't let your profession be an obstacle to knowing and loving your family."[12]

*Step #10*

# DECIDE TO STAY

B EFORE I BEGIN STEP #10, I need to say this: divorce is a necessary evil. Some marriages must be dissolved, for important, obvious reasons—such as addiction, abuse, and chronic adultery. There's also a myriad of psychological issues that, left untreated, can wreak havoc on a marriage. But in 1969, something happened to divorce.

As governor of California, Ronald Reagan signed the nation's first no-fault divorce legislature. Come the early 1970s, all but five states had adopted like bills and, as a result, all over the United States divorces skyrocketed. It was a free-for-all of commit with no consequences. And, as Reagan would later tell his son, it was "one of the worst mistakes he ever made in public office." Why? Because while it had good intent, no-fault divorce opened to the door to the casual and easy divorce culture we have today. The only "grounds" a divorcing couple needs to report is "irreconcilable differences."

That's a serious can of worms we opened. And it's the reason divorce has become a bona fide trend. No one likes to think of it this way, but at some point we have to say to ourselves, "Wait a minute. Something huge has happened." It's like the obesity epidemic: something fundamental has changed—for the worse. It's not like there's something in the water.

Here are some facts to shock us into reality. Research by sociologist James H. Fowler found that if a sibling divorces, we are 22 percent more likely to get divorced ourselves. And when our friends get divorced, it's even more influential: people who had a divorced friend were *147 percent* more likely to get divorced than people whose friends' marriages were intact.[1] Divorce, it appears, is contagious.

There's more. Studies show that of all divorcing couples, roughly half are open to staying together *if someone could tell or show them how to do so.* Um, that's a critical piece of information. It tells us millions of marriages are indeed salvageable. Now, I'm no marriage counselor, as you know. And this twelve-step program isn't designed to cover the myriad of problems married couples may face over their lifetime. But being silent about divorce because we're not experts or because we're afraid of stepping on people's toes does none of us any good. It doesn't solve the problem—it perpetuates it.

If I had my way, I'd like to be able to say something like this: "If you do all these things, you will live happily ever after . . ." But obviously, I can't say that. What I *can* do is tell you a few things I believe will help keep divorce at bay. The first is to follow Step #1 religiously: *Ignore the culture and live an examined life.* Because when it comes to getting married and staying married, the culture will steer you wrong every time.

Not long ago I was perusing the magazine section at an airport gift shop and noticed that headline after headline touted the single life for women. Being single is no longer considered a temporary state but something to which women should aspire. Women's magazines in particular are geared to this demographic, as are sitcoms and dramas. The programs repeatedly make fun of men and of being married to men. Even morning news programs chime in. When a nation of women see high-profile women basking in the single life and treating their husbands with disrespect or even disdain, eventually they assume this is normal. Before you know it, they start doing the same thing.

As I stared at these magazines, the first thing I thought of was how easy it is to lure people away from the more challenging road (marriage) and steer them toward the easy road (singlehood). It's human nature to travel the path of least resistance—and being single is, unquestionably, the path of least resistance. The choice to love and commit to another person for a lifetime is, as marriage guru Maggie Gallagher once wrote, "a much higher ideal than choosing not to."[2]

Being single doesn't ask people to look in the mirror and face their weaknesses in order to become better people. It doesn't require them to derail their plans to accommodate the needs of others. It doesn't expect people to learn the art of patience because they won't need to. Being single doesn't ask much of anyone. Single people can live however they see fit, with zero compromise. And now that society celebrates this lifestyle, it becomes all the more enticing to choose it.

The second thing you can do to keep divorce at bay is to *assume it isn't an option*. Remember when I said I freaked out before I married Chris because of my reservations? And the two of us concluded we could always get divorced? Talk about a self-fulfilling prophecy! If you haven't even gotten married and are already thinking of a way out, or if you're depending on a way out to relieve you of your commitment, you're doomed. Entering a marriage knowing you can always get out of it dramatically affects the way you approach the marriage itself.

Change your attitude, and you change the outcome. Assume there's no way out, and your chances of success improve exponentially. Remember what Barry Schwartz wrote? "When we can change our minds about decisions, we are less satisfied with them. When a decision is final, we engage in a variety of psychological processes that enhance our feelings about the choice we made relative to the alternatives."[3]

This psychological process applies to any choice we make. Whether you're deciding which car, television, or jeans to buy, or whether you're deciding whom to marry, make your decision as though you have no other option—as though it were your one and only shot. I cannot stress the significance of this attitude enough. It really is the whole enchilada.

When my husband and I have a conflict, even a big one, the prospect of divorce never enters our minds. If we gave ourselves this wiggle room, it would change the way we approach the problem. The best thing to do is accept going into a marriage that you're going to have problems—and that divorce is not the answer to those problems. If you can do that, you're well on your way to a successful marriage.

Not long ago, I had a conversation with a sixty-something wife and mother named Sally. Sally has been married to her husband for forty-four years, and when I asked her what she thinks the problem is with the modern generation—why they can't get the marriage thing right—she didn't hesitate. "They don't know what a vow is." Everything, she said, is disposable. If something isn't working, people throw it out.

Buck this trend.

Here's an idea to get you thinking outside the cultural box. When you find Mr. Right and you've been married for some time, pretend you're both stranded on an island. Assume you have no other choice but to work things out, and see if this doesn't change the way you approach your relationship. Clearly, you're not stuck. The point is to do the psychological work that's necessary to stay together.

All I'm suggesting, really, is that you start to look at choice in a whole new light. In modern America, choice is hailed as the be-all and end-all. "It's all about choice," we're told. Without choice, where would women be? The real answer: maybe better off.

Choice isn't all it's cracked up to be. In and of itself, it's good. But too much choice *can* be bad, as I touched upon earlier. When people have too much choice, says Schwartz, "bad stuff happens." [4] First, people become paralyzed. With so many options before them, people "can't pull the trigger." Instead of feeling liberated, they become immobilized.

In other words, too much choice causes people to develop inertia. They become so overwhelmed they don't know which choice to make. And those who *are* able to make a choice from the endless array of options before them often choose badly. "People make bad decisions even in simple environments. Just imagine how difficult the decisions are when the environments get complex." [5]

Finally, those who do end up choosing from all the options and choose *well* tend to become dissatisfied down the road. Choice has a bell curve, says Schwartz. People need to figure out for themselves at what point in the "choice space" they can derive the benefits of choice without the psychological loss. They need to find "the sweet spot." [6]

This process can be applied to any choice we make, including whom to marry. When people get divorced and remarry, unless the first choice was exceptionally bad (and certainly that happens), they end up with the same bell curve of happiness. Unfortunately, many people who get divorced don't change their thinking when they enter marriage the second time—which is one of the reasons second marriages are more precarious than first marriages.

At some point, people need to find their "sweet spot" or they'll end up divorced again and again. Either that, or they'll just give up and stay single. Remember: doubting your choice is perfectly normal. *Everyone does.* There is nothing wrong with you if, on some off day, you can't remember why the heck you married your husband in the first place. But if you never find your sweet spot, you'll end up like Kathleen Kinmont.

Kinmont, an actress we've both never heard of, wrote an article for the *HuffPo* titled, "The 'Do I Really Need a Man?' Checklist." Here's a portion of that article.

> It's been six months since my third husband moved out. After noting all the feelings and extra workload, I've decided to make a personal checklist of things I need from a man and things I don't . . .
>
> A few days after the ex moved out, I was so filled with anxiety thinking, "How am I going to manage taking care of the back and front yard by myself?" Thankfully, I was driving by a gardener when this heart palpitation started. I gasped, flagged him down, got his card and gave him my address. The next day he and his partner showed up, and what took my ex all weekend, every weekend, took them half an hour on a Thursday morning. They mowed and blew all my worry into the "yard waste only" can, and I was able to sleep like a baby again.
>
> Check off "I need a man to take care of the yard."
>
> So what about sex? I love it. I think it's really important. I just don't feel like I need a partner to help me pull it off. Certainly with all of the STDs out there, I'm not interested in getting anything else I don't already have.
>
> Check off "I need a man for sex." Just keep the electricity bill paid and all is good.
>
> Speaking of bills . . . do I really need a man to help me pay for them? No. I need a job to help me pay my bills. So to all you women out there in a good marriage or a bad one, get a paying job. It will help if things go awry. As soon as I get one, I'll check it off the list.
>
> I guess the last thing would be companionship. Can I just say that I'm chock full of it? I am on hyper overload with relationships. I have a wonderful family and great close friends that I barely have enough time for. I have more "friends," thanks to Facebook, than I know what to do with.
>
> I know that now is the time to fall in love with me, and remind myself that I was a whole person before I met "my other halves or quarters." I just have to fill in my fear with trust, and have the faith that exclaims, Yes, I am enough, and I can do this without a man as my guide or as my barometer of success.[7]

If Kinmont's story seems extreme, and I suppose it is (you probably don't have too many friends who've been married three times), it's relevant. Because this attitude, or some form of it, is precisely what many women feel about men and marriage. It's also the attitude that's portrayed in the media, thus perpetuating the notion that it's perfectly normal to think this way. Meanwhile, the truth lies buried: this woman is broken. Her conclusion after all that heartbreak is that she needs to fall in love with *herself*.

How sad is that?

I can't tell you how many men I hear from who want to be married but can't find a woman who, even if her attitude isn't quite as extreme as Kinmont's, *doesn't* talk just like this. I mentioned before that two-thirds of all divorces are initiated by women. There are two ways to read this: there really are no good men anymore, or there are no good men anymore because there are no good women.

My research tells me it's the latter.

I want you to consider a time in your life when you truly committed to something. When you said you were going to do it and you followed through, no matter how hard it was. Maybe you ran a half marathon, went on a diet, or penned a book. While there were probably times when you felt like giving up, how thankful are you that you powered through? That your word was your bond? I could be wrong, but my gut tells me that those moments when you made the decision to stay committed probably ended up being among the most rewarding moments of your life. Marriage is like riding a bicycle: you don't fall off unless you stop pedaling.

So break away from the pack. Assume it's workable. Decide to stay.

*Step #11*

# KNOW GOD, KNOW PEACE

THERE'S NO WAY TO WRITE a book about marriage and leave God out of the equation. But this a big subject, obviously; so I'm going to do my best to address it in just a few pages—and in a way I believe everyone can relate to, regardless of religious affiliation. You could pretty much sum up my advice this way: Being in a marriage without God is like showering without soap. You can do it, but the result won't be nearly as satisfying.

As you know, marriage is about sharing your life with someone else's. The moment you say, "I do," you will have joined forces with another human being and will presumably create new human beings. And when you do, life will no longer be about you. In fact, your needs will be last on the list. That's a tall order, especially for today's generation.

Previous generations didn't struggle as much in this regard. Moral relativity was a foreign concept; religion was an integral part of life; and people didn't have the distractions you and I do, the ones that pull us away from a life of sacrifice, toward a life of self-fulfillment.

We may consider it a boon that technology has made life so easy, but it has a huge downside in that it pulls us further and further away from sacrifice. And sacrifice is the only path to happiness. When we ignore this fact, we are left with a void. "Happiness is not a solitary endeavor; it's a joint enterprise, something that can only be created by the whole.

Contentment arises from a sense of family, community, and connectedness. Such virtues are in dwindling supply in America," wrote John Perry Barlow in *Forbes*.[1]

Consider the messages women have been sent about how to live a happy life. "Put yourself first." "Be empowered." "Don't lose yourself in marriage." "Find good child care." "Don't cater to your husband."

Do you think God would say any of these things?

No wonder the modern generation is chronically dissatisfied—sacrifice escapes them. Without the lessons of God and religion, which are ultimately about sacrifice, we humans would merely exist alongside each other, with no sense of obligation. The ability to give without recognition, to sacrifice, is what marriage is all about. And it will be *very* hard to do this without God.

In America, faith and religion have taken a nosedive. It is rare to find a wedding today in which God takes center stage. But have you noticed that at the same time religion has declined the divorce rate has gone up?

We've been hearing a lot these past few years about why people should get married at all. The world has changed, people say. Folks live longer, and women are economically independent. These things change the rules! Perhaps they do. But marriage is more than just a convenient arrangement. It is ultimately about learning how to love unconditionally. And love is universal: everyone wants to love and be loved. Without love, life is a just a series of hellos and good-byes.

That's where God comes in.

It's just impossible to love someone, *really* love someone, without God. Humans are fallible, weak, and selfish by nature—the presence of God makes us less so. That's not to say you can't find a selfless atheist. But it's rare. A recent study by the Chronicle of Philanthropy found that residents in states where religious participation is higher than the rest of the nation gave the greatest percentage of their discretionary income to charity. Indeed, every person I know who lacks faith—and I admit I don't know a ton—is inherently self-centered: they can't think outside their own wants and needs. When that's the case, love becomes an exercise in futility.

There's also this. It isn't a coincidence that at the same time life became infinitely easier, love became exponentially harder. When life is good, as it has been for decades (relatively speaking), faith isn't necessary.

Faith kicks in only when life gets difficult, or when bad things happen. But technology—and, until recently, a strong economy—has made life a piece of cake. The modern generation has grown up in an age of abundance; they have no idea what it means to sacrifice or do without. Without sacrifice, life is *too* good. Ergo, faith is unnecessary.

When it comes to lasting love, faith is critical. *The difference in the worldviews of someone who has faith and someone who lacks faith is huge.* Faith, or a lack thereof, is the prism through which we view the world and the people in it. If two people don't agree on this matter, they're going to have a hard time building a life together.

When I was dating Chris, I thought he and I were of one mind on faith and religion. It seemed to us we'd been raised similarly: both our mothers were raised Catholic but ultimately rejected that religion. There also wasn't much praying going on in either household. At least not openly.

But there were plenty of differences I didn't see. For example, Chris was never baptized and had never been to church. Conversely, I was baptized Presbyterian—and my family went to church services on Easter and Christmas and sporadically throughout the year. I even graduated from Catholic school. (I know, I know. Long story.)

Suffice it to say, I've always believed in God. But Chris wasn't so sure. He wasn't an atheist or anything, just skeptical. Whenever I'd bring up God or church, he'd become visibly uncomfortable. In fact, when we first met, I was recovering from the death of a four-year-old girl I had babysat every week since she was born. I remember wanting to go to church each year on her birthday and asking Chris to go with me, but he'd always refuse. At the time I read this as lack of support, which of course it was. What didn't register was its significance. Chris was so utterly removed from God and faith, he couldn't even bring himself to *enter* a church.

Chris's discomfort with religion bothered me; but because he wasn't hateful about it—on the contrary, he was envious of people of faith—I wasn't concerned. Plus, I wasn't thinking about marriage during the early years of our courtship, so I didn't pay much attention to it. But later, when we got engaged, conversations about church would come up and once again he'd get uncomfortable. I remember bringing Chris to the church in St. Louis where we were to be married, and he was like a fish out of water.

All those years we were together, I was aware of his indifference toward matters of an ethical nature. There didn't seem to be—no, there *wasn't*—any force guiding him toward a clear sense of right and wrong. Eventually, I put two and two together. The reason Chris was like this was because he didn't believe in God. He lacked faith.

Faith is the anchor that keeps us grounded in the face of life's hardships or unexplained phenomena. It enables us to act selflessly. If you don't have faith in anything other than yourself and the physical world, selfishness is a given and life is meaningless. Without God, people struggle to make sense of things and never feel content or satisfied. The physical world leaves people feeling lost and longing for more. The spiritual world, on the other hand, fills us up.

There's another reason your marriage needs God: children. Your kids are going to have questions, such as "Who's God?" or "How did we get here?" Children need something—Some*one*—other than their parents to answer to. This becomes abundantly clear the older children get.

Do yourself a favor and marry a man of faith. This is especially important if you're anything like me and your religious background wasn't set in stone. My husband is Catholic and has a strong faith. That we both attended Catholic schools explains why we're of the same mind, but that's not to say we always agree. The important thing is that one partner takes the lead. In my marriage, that person is my husband.

For the record, I'm not suggesting that in order to be a good person you have to be religious. Many people have a Kantian or Ayn Rand-esque view of the world, a philosophy that defends personal responsibility and a general "do unto others" approach to life. The problem there is that it's difficult to impart this philosophy to children.

Teaching a faith in God and taking part in daily prayer helps children endure things they cannot understand. It also helps them rely on someone other than Mom and Dad, which is important since their parents aren't always going to be there. Children also need to learn that people grow by surviving life's hardships—this is the core of our physical journey. Parents who have faith and use prayer teach children the tools they need to overcome difficult times and appreciate life's gifts.

Once again, modern culture has failed you in this regard, which is why (once again) you'll have to ignore the culture and live an examined life. You've grown up in a society where the existence of God is questioned at every turn. Atheism has become a "religion" of its own. Had you been born earlier, you would have known a different world, one where God was assumed to be an essential part of everyday life.

You would have had a clear and undeniable anchor.

You may laugh about this (you wouldn't be the first), but my husband and I have raised our children on a steady diet of *Little House on the Prairie* and *The Waltons*. We did this not to create a false and pretty image of life in those days; we're as thankful as anyone else to live in the modern age. But the lessons these programs impart—hard work, respect for one's parents, and *love of God*—are timeless and universal. No matter what day and age we live in, these messages are relevant. But they're not going to be taught by pop culture. If you want your children to know God, you have to know Him yourself. If you don't, they likely won't either.

Ultimately, faith means believing in something bigger than yourself. You are not the center of the universe. God is. If you know Him, you will find peace not only within yourself but with your husband as well.

And that *is* the goal, isn't it?

*Step #12*

# LEARN HOW TO BE A WIFE: WHAT DO YOU BRING TO THE TABLE?

WELL, WE'RE ALMOST THERE. NOW that you know how to choose a husband and create the life you want (and remember: these two cannot be extricated), it's time to focus on what it means to be a wife. What are *you* going to offer *him*? I don't know if you've thought about marriage in these terms, but it's important you do.

It took me years—seriously, years—to come to this conclusion, but there really is an art to being a wife. And trust me, I haven't mastered it. I'm always learning something new, and I've been a wife for almost twenty years! That's the thing about marriage. It is a continual act of refinement: your learning how to be a better wife, and his learning how to be a better husband. None of us is born with this skill. So on that note, allow me to share everything I've learned the hard way about being a wife.

There are sooooo many things to tell you—and of them all, the most important is this: *unless you marry a cad, what you bring to the marriage table may very likely determine the fate of your marriage.* Put another way: it's not what your guy can do for you, but what you can do for your guy. That's the attitude you need going forward.

Now before you charge back with, "What? Why should the strength of my marriage fall on my shoulders? Doesn't my husband have a role to play?" Indeed he does. But the male/female dance has a specific choreography; and the sooner you learn it, the better off you'll be. Wives have always been the arbiters of the marriage relationship. You've heard the phrase, "If Mama ain't happy, no one's happy." I can't tell you how true this is. Your demeanor really does set the stage.

That may sound like a lot of pressure, but it isn't really. It's just a matter of getting your head around it. Being married isn't nearly as difficult as you've been led to believe—most men are supremely easy to get along with. If you treat your husband well, he will be your greatest supporter and defender. If you treat him poorly, he'll either bark (my husband's a barker), or he'll hang his head and walk away. Wives have much more power than they realize.

Below are my top six tricks of the trade—aka "things Suzanne learned the hard way." Try them on for size, although they may sound foreign to you. In fact, I'm sure they will. But once you roll them around on your tongue awhile, you will find they make all the sense in the world. Maybe not at first.

But eventually.

## 1. PUT DOWN YOUR SWORD

I honestly believe there's so much unnecessary marital strife today for one simple reason: women are bitter. They're defensive; they're competitive; and they're ready to pounce.

It's not their fault, really. They've been taught that women all over the world (as if America is no different from Third World countries) have been passed over and subjugated for centuries. It's second nature for modern women to ward off men who they believe will hold them down so there's nothing left but some half-baked version of a former self.

Because of this assumption about men and marriage, equality is always the goal. Women want to prove they're strong and capable and can't be messed with. To them, that's power. But all women end up doing is proving to men how angry they are. And who wants to be with someone who's mad all the time?

I hate to be the bearer of bad news, but the tools you've been given for success in the workforce are the exact same tools that will screw up your marriage. (Remember when I said power and love are at odds?) If you want to be in charge at work, fine. Get it out of your system. But when you get home, put down your sword. Surrender. Your husband doesn't want to control you. He just wants to love you and take care of you.

Let him.

## 2. BE SWEET (OR, BECOME ONE WITH YOUR INNER FEMININE)

The second thing you'll need to do as a wife is be sweet. Consider Audrey Hepburn. Have you ever seen a woman who acts like Audrey Hepburn? I haven't, and it's unfortunate, because so many relationships could be salvaged if women were simply *nicer* to men.

Women today are mean. And what makes this phenomenon so sad is that if women learned how to embrace their femininity and use it to their advantage, they could have the love they want. But women have been taught that being sweet means being clueless (consider the image people have of June Cleaver or Jackie Kennedy), so their knee-jerk reaction is to chuck their feminine proclivities. This has resulted in a generation of, for lack of a better word, bitches.

It wasn't that long ago that being bitchy was considered a negative quality. Today it's considered a positive trait. Countless movies and television programs associate female strength with bitchiness. There was even a book published in 2002 called *Why Men Love Bitches*—which was very successful. The author, Sherry Argov, claimed the term *bitch* means the opposite of being a doormat.

But there's nothing new about teaching women not to be doormats—and it shouldn't be confused with being *bitchy*, which is a negative term. Being a doormat means having no life or interests of your own, and that kind of relationship would cause anyone to feel smothered or caged. Not being a doormat means being like Elizabeth in *Pride and Prejudice* as opposed to her sister, Lydia, who's so dumb and desperate Wickham walks all over her.

The alternative to being like Lydia is not to become a "bitch," which simply translates to being aggressive, demanding, and difficult. Elizabeth would never have earned Darcy's "affections" had she been a bitch. Yet she was certainly a woman in her own right. *Being strong and confident is not the same thing as being a bitch.*

The confusion about women's strength vs. weakness is a result of people's perception of the 1950s housewife: that she was a doormat. (Hence the theme of *Why Men Love Bitches*: down with the dumb housewife, up with the empowered woman who doesn't take crap from a man.) But 1950s housewives weren't doormats. On the contrary, they understood men and the marriage relationship.

To explain this concept further, consider this Facebook comment a twenty-something male posted in response to a woman who said she felt honored to be the Other Woman in her man's life because his wife was one of those "submissive" types.

> That man isn't cheating with you cause you are so good at being the other woman . . . he's cheating with you cause you aren't good enough to be THE woman. Learn what submission really means. A submissive woman is far from weak cause a true submissive woman knows how to carry the load for him and her both without him even having to know it. She knows how to speak to his spirit and not his lusts. She knows how to push him to his dreams instead of pulling him to destruction. She knows how to pray with him and not play with him. She knows how to be quiet even when her flesh wants to speak. She knows the value of his hard work and not just his dollar. A submissive woman is his "LIFETIME" but you are just a "GOOD TIME" . . . and that's all you will ever be.

I'm sure you've heard the phrase, "You'll attract more bees with honey than you will with vinegar." This is the very aspect of human nature against which feminists have rebelled. To them, being sweet means being a doormat. *They are wrong.* Being feminine—kind, soft, nurturing, or whatever adjective you prefer—is only suffocating if you're in love with a Neanderthal.

But you know what? I've never actually met a Neanderthal, and I'm almost forty-five. I'm sure he exists, but he can't be the norm or I would have met him by now. Most men are much nicer than feminists would have you believe. And if you treat them with honey as opposed to vinegar, you'd be surprised what you'll get in return.

Men's desire to love, honor, and protect women is instinctive. Do you remember the recent movie theater massacre when a man named

James Holmes murdered twelve people (and injured fifty-eight more) in
Aurora, Colorado? Three men—Jon Blunk, Matt McQuinn, and Alex
Teves—died shielding their girlfriends from Holmes's rampage.[1] I don't
know about you, but I don't want men like that to disappear.

Men can smell femininity a mile away; its energy is a magnet. When
you and I walk past a group of men sitting in conversation, 99 percent of
the time these men will stop talking and look up. That's not because we're
gorgeous (well, I can only speak for myself)—it's because we're female.
Indeed, women have *unbelievable* power over men.

They've simply misused it.

Maybe women think being bitchy is attractive since that's what *they're*
attracted to. Women love guys who aren't sweet. They gravitate toward
men who are confident, accomplished, and yes, even full of themselves.
Women are forever passing up the nice guy in favor of the jerk. But you
can rarely turn this scenario around. Men don't want a bitch for a wife.
So don't be one.


## 3. DON'T DRIVE THE BUS

When it comes to being a wife, deference is key. *Deference* means a cour-
teous regard for, or respect toward, another person's opinions or judgment. Modern women don't like to be deferential. They associate it with
being subservient to men, and if there's one thing American women pride
themselves on, it's being independent and in charge. When channeled
properly, in the workforce for example, these qualities can work well. In
a romantic relationship, they're the kiss of death.

Marriages in which only one person drives the bus are the marriages
with the best chance of survival. The man doesn't *always* have to be the
driver; but in most cases, that's what works. I know putting it in these terms
riles people's feathers. But submission, or surrendering control, is not the
same as subservience. The latter connotes inferiority—the former does not.

Do you remember when Michele Bachmann was asked during a
Republican debate whether or not as president she'd be submissive to her
husband? The question was in response to a comment Bachmann had
made back in 2006. In describing her career as a tax lawyer, she told an
audience she wasn't all that interested in tax law, but her husband sug-

gested she pursue it as a career. To which Mrs. Bachmann added, "The Lord says, 'Wives, you are to be submissive to your husbands.'"[2] So she became a tax attorney.

I admit it was a poor choice of words if she was hoping to gain widespread appeal to women. Any reference to the Bible or to wives being submissive to their husbands ignites apoplexy in most women. But you don't have to be a Bible thumper to appreciate the purpose of submission. To submit means to surrender. And surrendering *unnecessary* control is, ironically, liberating.

Take me, for instance. I tend to be a control freak. I like things the way I like them—and if I want something done right, I do it myself. This quality has been great for the marketplace, but it's terrible for my marriage. For example, I used to tell my husband how to drive all the time, and he couldn't stand it. I also wanted to decide where we'd go for dinner. I didn't trust he'd make the right plan, or even *any* plan for that matter—even though he's perfectly aware of the restaurants I like. Today, I find it liberating to go out for dinner and let my husband choose the place, and I'm much better about keeping my mouth shut about his driving.

I actually *love* being a passenger now. If I'm feeling really crazy, I leave my purse at home because that makes me feel even less in control! Between my work and my kids (and my mother, who lives with us), I'm in charge all the time. When I'm with my husband, I don't want to be in charge. So I surrender.

Another problem that arises in marriages in which two people try to take charge is the need to be right all the time. But needing to be right just for the sake of being right is the opposite of love. In fact, needing to be in control is nothing more than fear—fear that you won't get what you want. But if you choose (or chose) the right husband, your ability to surrender will be greatly rewarded. You husband isn't going to hurt you, walk all over you, or control you. He *will* take care of your needs, but you have to let him. Men don't like to fight with women—and when two people try to drive the bus, fighting is inevitable. That's why you need to surrender.

Sadly, modern women have no tools for this dynamic—no clue how to step back and let men take charge. To them, the mere idea sounds appalling. That's because they've been taught that *not* being in control means losing one's identity or becoming a doormat.

Nothing could be further from the truth.

Speaking of surrendering, let's go back to *Fifty Shades of Grey*. Remember, I said the book's underlying theme is trust and submission. Once Anastasia gets past her initial fear of being controlled by a man, she finds she likes surrendering. Somewhere deep down, where feminists can't reach, women are happiest when they're *not* in control—at least when it comes to love. Most women like the men in their lives to be dominant. They want to bury their heads in a big, strong chest and feel protected. That was the theme of *Fifty Shades of Grey*, and women absorbed it like a sponge.

## 4. HAVE SEX

"Ours is now a terribly under-sexed society. I have talked to a lot of young women about this, and they just don't seem to do it any more. Honestly. I suppose it's because we all have so many other demands on our time now."[3] So says romance novelist Jilly Cooper.

It's true married sex has taken a nosedive, which we know only because women are so outspoken today about their sex lives. I'm reminded of a conversation I had with a woman I know named Laura. Laura is a forty-nine-year-old physical therapist. She's petite, with long, wavy, dark hair and beautiful skin—think Giada De Laurentiis. She told me that not one but *several* of her friends confided in her that they rarely sleep with their husbands. There was nothing wrong with these men, she said—they were great husbands, and not unattractive or overweight. Their wives just didn't feel like having sex and didn't think they should have to.

Laura was despondent upon hearing this and didn't know what to say. Should she tell her friends how wrong it is? She wasn't sure. She and I had a long conversation about what's going on with relationships these days. When I told Laura how so many women are mired in the me-first, empowered feminist worldview, she was genuinely perplexed. It's so easy to take care of a husband, she said. What's the problem? Just be nice, cook, and have sex!

Have you heard of the Pioneer Woman? You know, from that show on the Food Network about the cowboy wife and her kids? Her real name's Ree Drummond, and she wrote a book called *The Pioneer Woman: Black Heels to Tractor Wheels—A Love Story*.[4] It's basically a memoir.

Ree Drummond was born in Oklahoma but moved to California to go to college, where she soaked up her vegetarian, freewheelin' lifestyle like a sponge. After graduation, Drummond's career took off. Getting married and having babies were the last things on her mind. But on her way back from Los Angeles, en route to Chicago, she stopped in her hometown, where she met a devastatingly masculine cowboy she calls "Marlboro Man." A relationship ensued, and eventually Marlboro Man asked Drummond to marry him. A rancher with deep roots in the land he works, he had no intention of leaving his ranch—so Drummond decided to give up her independent, footloose life in the big city to become a rancher's wife. Today, the Pioneer Woman and her Marlboro Man have four children.

The reason I'm sharing her story is because throughout the book, Drummond made several references to her formerly feminist self. More than once, she wrote about how she'd had to get of rid of the feminist thoughts that had infected her mind. The ones that told her she shouldn't give up her dreams for a man, that she should never fall for a strapping fella and rearrange her entire life plans as a result. Strong, powerful women don't swoon.

Yet swoon Drummond did. And the sexual energy she described as a result of surrendering her feminist disposition was palpable. Drummond's story is a fantastic illustration of how feminism pulls women away from their natural feminine instincts and steers them toward a false notion of empowerment. It's also proof that masculinity and femininity are a potent combination.

I would also note that giving up her feminist compulsions and succumbing to human nature did not oppress Drummond in the least. She has a wildly successful website and her own television show. I don't know her personally; but based on her writing, this is a woman who understands that the face she wears at work cannot be the same face she wears at home.

Men don't want the work face at home. They're disarmed by women's aggressive, controlling, and demanding ways. They don't want a competitor *or* a doormat. They want a wife who isn't needy, yes—but they don't want a wife who doesn't need them.

See the difference?

## 5. KEEP YOURSELF FIT

I recently saw an article in the *Ladies' Home Journal* called "What Happily Married Couples Do." One of the things it said was that married couples who put an effort into their appearance have more active lives—and better sex. That's hardly surprising. If each of us has to live with, look at, and have sex with the same person every day for decades, the least we can do is give our partners something good to work with! I'm not saying people need to be beautiful or have perfect bodies; I just mean they shouldn't stop trying to look their best just because they caught a fish.

This is not advice our politically correct culture appreciates. A marriage counselor I know once told me that when she was a guest on *Oprah*, one of the husbands on the panel expressed dismay over his wife's weight gain and admitted he was less attracted to her. When the counselor supported the husband's request that his wife lose weight, she practically got her head cut off.

Oprah and the audience told the marriage counselor how terrible it was that she would suggest a wife lose weight in order to be more attractive to her husband. That she suggested husbands do the same didn't matter. The implication was clear: women should be able to let themselves go, and their husbands should just get over it. Any other attitude amounts to oppression.

People embrace this same victim mentality when husbands have affairs, even though when husbands cheat they're usually suffering in the marriage just as wives are when *they* cheat. The difference is that when husbands cheat, they're publicly chastised. When wives cheat, it's assumed their husbands drove them to it.

Yes, there are men like Hugh Grant and Jesse James—but they're the exception, not the rule. Most of the time, good husbands stray because they feel rejected by their wives. But we're not allowed to acknowledge this because it means we're blaming the woman for her husband's transgression, even though addressing the *reasons* he strayed can actually resolve the underlying problem.

To even imply that wives may play a part in why husbands stray borders on blasphemy. But the truth is, every action has a reaction. Rather than view it as "husband perpetrator/wife victim," we should ask ourselves what went wrong in the first place. Plenty of marriages survive after an infidelity. But it takes work—and if the wife views herself as a perpetual victim, the wound will never heal. Same goes for the husband.

It's important to note, too, that men and women cheat for different reasons. Husbands often cheat when the opportunity presents itself (remember: men can separate sex from emotion), and they haven't had sex with their wives in a long time. For wives, the circumstances are a bit different. "By the time a woman is at the point of physically cheating with another man, she has often emotionally vacated her primary relationship," writes sex therapist Ian Kerner.[5] When this happens, women can become vulnerable to the first man who starts paying them some attention.

Both scenarios (why men cheat and why women cheat) stem from the same issue—a desire to be loved and accepted—but their means of connection differ: for men, it's sex; for women, it's communication. I've also noticed that when wives cheat, husbands will often admit they screwed up and sent their wives into the arms of another man. I don't think I've ever heard a wife be that generous.

6. TALK LESS; LISTEN MORE

My final piece of advice is to talk less and listen more. These days, communication is hailed as The Answer to a great relationship, but it's overrated. I agree communication is key in that you don't want to hold back your feelings, or you'll blow up later. But there really is such a thing as too much communication. Take it from someone who often needs to be reminded of this fact: there are going to be plenty of times in your marriage when the best thing you can do for your relationship is Shut Up.

Silence can be very powerful. When I say nothing as opposed to something, I often find I've said a lot. That may be because my husband's so used to hearing me talk that my silence has become ultra-powerful. Think about a time when your guy said something that made you mad or embarrassed you. When this happens, the urge to speak can be overwhelming. But if you can muster the courage—the *deference*—to keep still, trust me: you will have spoken volumes.

Men often know what their wives or girlfriends are thinking because we talk so much more than they do. Because of this, they sometimes need to tune us out. This is annoying, I know, but it also means that when we don't say anything, they hear that silence loud and clear. (Sort of like when men finally *do* say something, we women perk up.) So when I say communication is overrated, I don't mean you should hold all your thoughts and feelings inside and never let them out.

I just mean sometimes you should.

So that's my best advice about being a wife; I hope it's helpful. Just remember that being a wife (and husband, for that matter) is a work in progress. It's a role that requires a great deal of maturity and self-reflection. Whatever you do, do not assume you're always the victim—you have a role to play in the dynamics of your marriage. To resolve whatever issues arise, it's critical that you're able to look in the mirror. Marriage is a two-way street.

Good luck on your journey.

*Epilogue*

HOW TO CHOOSE A HUSBAND has been a difficult book to write—for a lot of reasons. If you recall, at the beginning I said I don't have all the answers. That's worth repeating: I don't have all the answers. Marriage is complicated business.

Still, something must be done. According to Pew Research Center, the share of men ages eighteen to thirty-four that say having a successful marriage is one of the most important things in their lives has *dropped* six percentage points since 1997, from 35 percent to 29 percent. For women, the opposite has occurred: the share voicing this opinion *rose*, from 28 percent to 37 percent. Put another way: Despite the focus on America's new crop of single women, it appears women still want to marry. But men don't.

Over the past few years I've heard from scores of men and women, both here and abroad, and their views on marriage support the study above. Men have made it clear they're not interested in getting married. And they've told me why: women aren't women anymore. As a result of this phenomenon, many men are looking outside the United States for brides who are openly solicitous of their desire for a traditional family.

For months, writers and journalists have been asking where all the good men have gone. The answer is simple: American women changed the rules. They began to sleep around and shack up with their boyfriends under the guise that women are just as disinterested in commitment as men are. That's baloney.

It's also a foolish course of action, as women have now depleted the pool of marriageable men. Men tend to follow women's lead—they always have. When women lower their standards, they get lesser lives in return. If they turn things around, if they *raise* their standards, marriageable men will reappear.

If you want love in your life, you have to earn it. So change your attitude, ladies. Do the right thing. Lead the way.

One final note before I leave you. In Step #9, I talked about the "having it all" syndrome that plagues modern women. I said my choice of career is much more doable for a wife and mother than many other careers. And that's true—it is. Still, even I am not exempt from the fallout. Writing this book took a toll on my family life in a way writing hadn't before.

Throughout the year it took to complete, we sold our home and moved my eighty-two-year-old mother out of the home she had lived in for forty-five years and in with us. Then my husband hurt his back and was out of commission for a month. Then my mother-in-law died. Then school let out for the summer, and I had to "work" for about a month in the summertime for the first time since I had children. Needless to say, I'm thrilled to get The Book off my plate. I'm tired of it taking up so much brain space.

Look, we all have a life outside of work. If it's full, and for most of us it is, our work *can't* consume us. I want to wake up early and roll over to my husband's side of the bed instead of getting up immediately to write a book. I want to have an organized kitchen again. I want to exercise more. I want to keep up with the news of the day. I want to cook better meals. I want to concentrate on what my friends are saying instead of taking in only half of the information. When you're raising children and trying to accomplish something else *equally taxing* at the same time, life is too crazy—even when the kids are older. I thought it would get easier, but it hasn't.

Bottom line: there are more important things in life than work. Like love. I have the most loving husband in the world. He's as committed to the message of this book as I am (and to my writing career in general) but like me, gets frustrated with the lack of time to get it all done. *Time*—not men, employers, or the way the system is rigged—is the real culprit when it comes to having it all. There just aren't enough hours in the day. That's why trying to maintain two demanding careers when you're married and raising a family is hopeless. Our brains aren't equipped to handle it, and our families weren't designed to withstand it.

My husband is genuinely thrilled I wrote this book, but he wants his wife back.

Now he can have her.

*Appendix*

# THE TOP 10 DO'S AND DON'TS OF BEING A WIFE

1.     When it isn't absolutely necessary to speak up, don't.

2.     Have sex with your husband whether you're in the mood or not. You'll probably change your mind once things get going.

3.     It's okay to cook for your husband and even—gasp—serve him a plate of food. Cooking is love.

4.     Encourage your husband to go out with the guys just as you like to go out with your girlfriends. (Note: This does not include an eight-hour game of golf on Saturday after you've just given birth.)

5.     If you're home with young children and your husband is the breadwinner, give him time to decompress after work. Don't shove a baby in his arms when he gets home and take off for the night.

6.     Do everything in your power not to measure the amount of work your husband does at home with the amount of work you do at home. If you're your children's primary caregiver, you will always do more household chores because you're simply around the house more. Unless your husband spends most of his time in front of the TV outside of work, he's probably pitching in more than you think. (See Step #9 for details.)

7.      Make your husband's family your family, particularly since you expect him to do likewise.

8.      Let your husband date you. This includes letting him choose where you'll be going, letting him drive, and allowing him to hold the door open for you. It also means letting him pay the bill. (Even though the money's in one pot, the gesture is important.)

9.      When you and your husband have a conflict, look in the mirror. You may or may not be to blame, but recognizing that what you're doing isn't working can help steer you in a different direction. You can't change other people—only yourself.

10.     Last, but definitely not least: Don't be a bitch. Be sweet.

*Notes*

PART I

## WHAT THIS BOOK IS

1. Eric Klinenberg, "One's a Crowd," *The New York Times*, February 4, 2012.
2. Rebecca Traister, "Love and the Single Girl," *Marie Claire*, June 2012.
3. Elizabeth Bernstein, "Divorcé's Guide to Marriage," *The Wall Street Journal*, July 24, 2012.
4. Lena Dunham to Frank Bruni, "The Bleaker Sex," *The New York Times*, March 31, 2012.
5. Hanna Rosin, "Sexual Freedom and Women's Success," *The Wall Street Journal*, March 23, 2012.
6. Janelle Nanos, "Single by Choice: Why More of Us Than Ever Before Are Happy to Never Get Married," *Boston Magazine*, January 2012.
7. Rachel Fine, "I Now Pronounce You . . . Girlie" *The Huffington Post*, October 20, 2011.
8. Kate Bolick, "All the Single Ladies," *The Atlantic*, November 2011.
9. Susan Gregory Thomas, "The Divorce Generation," *The Wall Street Journal*, July 9, 2011.
10. Ibid.

## CHAPTER 1: THE NAKED EMPEROR

1. Gloria Steinem, "Gloria in Her Own Words," HBO documentary, August 2011.
2. Sharyn Alfonsi, "Is Dad the New Mom? The Rise of Stay-at-Home Fathers," *ABC News*, June 18, 2012.
3. Brad LaRosa, "Sandra Bullock Ribs Street on Rivalry," ABC News, March 4, 2010.

## CHAPTER 2: NEVER RELY ON A MAN

1. Suzanne Venker, "Rich Women and Emasculated Men," *National Review*, April 2, 2012, http://www.nationalreview.com/home-front/295021/rich-women-and-emasculated-men/suzanne-venker.

## CHAPTER 3: SLUTVILLE

1. Mary Matalin, *Letters to My Daughters* (New York: Simon & Schuster, 2004), 45.
2. Tom Valeo, "Boy brain, meet girl brain," Tampabay.com, August 6, 2006, http://www.sptimes.com/2006/08/06/news_pf/Books/Boy_brain__meet_girl_.shtml.
3. Lawrence Spivak to Gloria Steinem, NBC News *Meet the Press*, September 10, 1972.

## CHAPTER 4: EXPECTATIONS

1. Laurie Wagner, *Expectations* (San Francisco: Chronicle Books, 1998), 33.
2. Anne-Marie Slaughter, "Women Still Can't Have It All," *The Atlantic*, July/August 2012.

## PART II

## STEP #1

1. Gordon MacDonald, *Ordering Your Private World* (Nashville: Thomas Nelson, 2007).
2. Ibid.
3. Myrna Blyth, *Spin Sisters: How the Women of the Media Sell Unhappiness and Liberalism to the Women of America* (New York: St. Martin's Press, 2004), vii.
4. Dani Klein Modisett, "My Kids Stole My Ambition!" *Huffington Post*, February 2, 2012.
5. Steve Jobs, commencement address, Stanford University (Stanford, CA), 2005.

## STEP #2

1. Jone Johnson Lewis, "Julia Child Quotes," About.com: Women's History, http://womenshistory.about.com/od/juliachild/a/julia_child_2.htm.
2. Charles R. Swindoll, ThinkExist.com Quotations, http://thinkexist.com/quotation/life_is-what_happens_to_you_and_how_you_react_to/158456.html.
3. Barry Schwartz, *The Paradox of Choice: Why More Is Less* (New York: Harper Collins, 2004), 142.
4. Rachel Lehmann-Haupt, "The Aniston Syndrome," Babble, July 19, 2010, http://www.babble.com/pregnancy/gettingpregnant
endnotes 5 and 6 should be as follows:
5. Ibid.
6. Ibid.

7. Second Acts, "Chef's Special: Cooking and Cruising," Wall Street Journal, July 12, 2012, http://online.wsj.com/article/SB10001424052702304840904577426544065238990.html.
8. Charles Murray, "Why Capitalism Has an Image Problem," Wall Street Journal, July 30, 2012.
9. David McCullough Jr., "David McCullough Jr.'s commencement address: You're Not Special," Boston Herald, June 7, 2012, http://bostonherald.com/news/regional/view/20120607youre_not_special.


STEP #3
1. Kris Fuchs, "Letting Go of the BlackBerry," The Wall Street Journal, March 27, 2012.
2. Louann Brizendine, The Female Brain (New York: Broadway Books, 2006), 12.
3. Ibid.
4. Kenneth Minogue, "Modern Love," The Wall Street Journal, March 10, 2012.
5. Wikiquote, s.v. "My Big Fat Greek Wedding," http://en.wikiquote.org/wiki/My_Big_Fat_Greek_Wedding.
6. Steve Harvey, Act Like a Lady, Think Like a Man (New York: Harper Collins, 2009), 180–81.
7. Sam Botta, interview with author. (May 2012)
8. Harvey, Act Like a Lady, 43.
9. See Brizendine, The Female Brain, [[insert page numbers; if this point is actually from both her books, add that: e.g., See Brizendine, The Female Brain, XX; The Male Brain, XX]].
10. Harvey, Act Like a Lady, 71–72.


STEP #4

1. Scarlett Online, Gone with the Wind Script Two, http://www.scarlettonline.com/gone_with_the_wind_script_2.htm
2. Maureen Dowd, "An Ideal Husband," The New York Times, July 26, 2008.
3. M. Scott Peck, The Road Less Traveled (New York: Simon & Schuster, 1978), 84.
4. Ibid., 85.
5. Ibid., 15.


STEP #5

1. Meg Jay, "The Downside of Cohabiting before Marriage," The New York Times Sunday Review (opinion pages), April 12, 2012, http://www.nytimes.com/2012/04/15/opinion/sunday/the-downside-of-cohabiting-before-marriage.html?pagewanted=all.
2. David Popenoe, "Cohabitation: The Marriage Enemy," USA Today, July 28, 2000.
3. Jay, "The Downside of Cohabiting before Marriage."
4. Schwartz, The Paradox of Choice, 228; emphasis added. (See Step #2, n. 3.)
5. George Gilder, Men and Marriage (Gretna, LA: Pelican Publishing, 1992), 187–88.


STEP #6

1. Rachel Weight, "How The Notebook Has Ruined Me," The Huffington Post, May 11, 2012, http://www.huffingtonpost.com/rachel-weight/the-notebook_b_1508359.html.
2. Po Bronson and Ashley Merryman, Nurtureshock: New Thinking about Children (New York: Twelve, 2009), 9.

3. Vicki Larson, "Why Women Walk Out More Than Men," *The Huffington Post*, January 24, 2011, http://www.huffingtonpost.com/vicki-larson/why-women-want-out-more-t_b_792133.html.
4. Schwartz, *The Paradox of Choice* (see Step #2, n. 3).
5. Ibid., 229.

## STEP #7

1. Kathryn Lopez, "Ann Romney, Everywoman" *National Review* (April 16, 2012)
2. Megan Rutherford, "When Mother Stays Home," *Time.com*, October 16, 2000, http://www.time.com/time/magazine/article/0,9171,998242,00.html.
3. Harvey, *Act Like a Lady, Think Like a Man*, 11. (See Step #1, n. 5.)
4. Liza Mundy, *The Richer Sex: How the New Majority of Female Breadwinners Is Transforming Sex, Love, and Family* (New York: Simon & Schuster, 2012), 2.
5. http://www.thefreedictionary.com/empower.
6. www.quotationspage.com/quote/137.html.

## STEP #8

1 Human Fertilisation and Embryology Authority, "Fertility Facts and Figures 2008," December 8, 2010, http://www.hfea.gov.uk/docs/2010-12-08_Fertility_Facts_and_Figures_2008_Publication_PDF.PDF, 10.
2. Ibid.
3. Rebecca Walker, "How my mother's fanatical views tore us apart," *Mail Online* (UK), May 23, 2008, http://www.dailymail.co.uk/femail/ article-1021293/How-mothers-fanatical-feminist-views-tore-apart- daughter-The-Color-Purple-author.html.
4. Miriam Grossman, "The Dangers of Social Ideology in Campus Health Care," *Policy Express*, no. 7-2, April 15, 2007, Clare Boothe Luce Policy Institute.
5. "Movie and TV Stars Become Mommies after 40," Squidoo, n.d. http://www.squidoo.com/Over40celebritymoms; accessed August 28, 2012.
6. "Brooke Shields: an advocate for fertility issues," Toronto Centre for Advanced Reproductive Technology, n.d., http://bodyandhealth.canada.com/channel_health_features_details.asp?health_feature_id=378&article_id=1200&channel_id=2048&relation_id=36904; accessed August 28, 2012.
7. Associated Press, "Courteney Cox Has Baby Girl," FoxNews.com, June 14, 2004, http://www.foxnews.com/story/0,2933,122604,00.html.
8. "Movie and TV Stars Become Mommies after 40."
9. Kate Fridkis, "The Invisible Baby That Follows Me Around," *Eat the Damn Cake* (blog), December 16, 2011, http://www.eatthedamncake.com/2011/12/16/the-invisible-baby-that-follows-me-around/.

## STEP #9

1. Jennifer Lopez, "Jennifer Lopez Talks Adoption, Life as a Single Mom and Having More Kids," *E! Online*, May 9, 2012.
2. Suzanne Venker, *7 Myths of Working Mothers* (Dallas: Spence Publishing, 2004), 158.
3. Kate Pickert, "Are You Mom Enough?" *Time*, May 21, 2012.

4. William and Wendy Dreskin, *The Daycare Decision* (New York: M. Evans and Company, Inc., 1983), 50.
5. Kitty Kelley, *Oprah: A Biography* (New York: Crown Publishers, 2010), 160.
6. Karl Zinsmeister, "The Problem with Daycare," *American Enterprise*, May/June 1998.
7. Nancy Gibbs, "What Women Want Now," *Time*, October 14, 2009.


8. Betsey Stevenson and Justin Wolfers, *The Paradox of Declining Female Happiness* (Working Paper 14969) (Cambridge, MA: National Bureau of Economic Research, 2009), http://www.nber.org/papers/w14969.pdf?new_window=1, p. 5.
9. "Transcript and Video of Speech by Sheryl Sandberg, Chief Operating Officer, Facebook," Barnard College commencement, New York City, May 17, 2011, http://barnard.edu/headlines/transcript-and-video-speech-sheryl-sandberg-chief-operating-officer-facebook.
10. Ibid.
11. Catharine Smith, "Facebook COO Sheryl Sandberg, 'I Feel Guilty Working Because of My Kids,'" *Huffington Post*, July 4, 2011, http://www.huffingtonpost.com/2011/07/04/facebook-coo-sheryl-sandberg-new-yorker_n_889768.html.
12. Iris Krasnow, *Surrendering to Motherhood: Losing Your Mind, Finding Your Soul* (New York: Miramax, 1998), 72.

## STEP #10

1. Stephanie Chen, "Could you be 'infected' by a friend's divorce?" *CNN Living*, June 10, 2010.
2. Maggie Gallagher, "The New Enemies of Eros," *National Review Online*, October 20, 2011.
3. Schwartz, *The Paradox of Choice*, 228; emphasis added. (See Step #2, n. 3.)
4. Barry Schwartz, "The Paradox of Choice" (talk), TED Conference, July 2005.
5. Ibid.
6. Ibid.
7. Kathleen Kinmont, "The 'Do I Really Need a Man?' Checklist," *HuffPost Divorce:* The Blog, http://www.huffingtonpost.com/kathleen-kinmont/life-after-divorce_b_1478051.html.

## STEP #11

1. John Perry Barlow, "The Pursuit of Emptiness: Why Americans Have Never Been a Happy Bunch," *Forbes*, December 3, 2001, 97.

## STEP #12

1. Alex Groberman, "Jon Blunk, Matt McQuinn, Alex Teves Died Trying to Save Girlfriends During Batman Movie Massacre," July 23, 2012, Opposing Views, http://www.opposingviews.com/i/society/crime/jon-blunk-matt-mcquinn-alex-teves-died-trying-save-girlfriends-during-batman-movie.
2. Michele Bachmann to Byron York, Republican National Debate, Iowa, August 12, 2011.
3. Jilly Cooper, "'Bonkbuster' is dead because women have lost their libidos," *Telegraph* (UK), June 24, 2012.
4. William Morrow, 2011.
5. Ian Kerner, "Fox on Sex: Why Women Cheat," September 13, 2010.

# Index

*Today Show*:  28, 82
Traister, Rebecca:  vii


**U**

UCLA:  87


**V**

View, The:  28


**W**

Wagner, Laurie:  19
Walker, Alice:  86
Walker, Rebecca:  86
*Wall Street Journal*:  viii, 28, 34, 39, 78
Walters, Barbara:  5
*Waltons, The*:  117
Weight, Rachel:  67
Whitehead, Barbara Dafoe:  60
Why Men Love Bitches:  121-122
Winfrey, Oprah:  101, 127
*Wonder of Boys, The*:  41
*Wonder of Girls, The*:  41


**Y**

Yahoo:  28, 98

In *The Flipside of Feminism*, Venker and Schlafly provide readers with a new view of women in America — one that runs counter to what Americans have been besieged with for decades. Their book demonstrates that conservative women are, in fact, the most liberated women in America and the folks to whom young people should be turning for advice. Their confident and rational approach to the battle of the sexes is precisely what America needs.

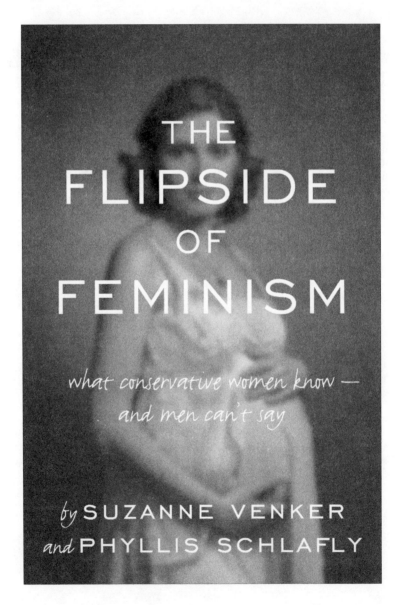

THE
FLIPSIDE
OF
FEMINISM

*what conservative women know —
and men can't say*

*by* SUZANNE VENKER
*and* PHYLLIS SCHLAFLY

 WND BOOKS

WND Books • a WND Company • Washington, DC • www.wndbooks.com

# No publisher in the world has a higher percentage of *New York Times* bestsellers.

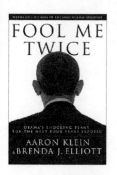

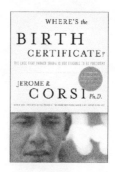
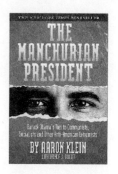

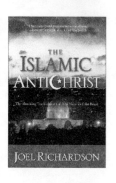

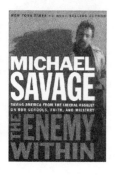
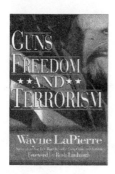
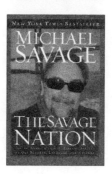